THE CITY MARKET

A Tale of Growing Up in a Tavern

C.P. Negri

The City Market
A Tale of Growing Up In A Tavern
By C.P. Negri

ISBN: 978-0-9819884-7-4

Printed in the United States of America.

For Kazu.

1

My family's business, the City Market, was only half truthful. The "city" was just a small town. When I was growing up, there wasn't a single building in the central business district over eight stories tall (there still isn't, actually). But technically it was a city.

The other part of the lie is that while our store was a market, the rear half was what is regionally referred to as a beer garden. You might know it as a gin mill, alehouse, pub, grog shop, tap house, or simply tavern. Even the term "beer garden" was not accurate, since it had no outdoor seating as in a real *bier garten* in Germany.

The fruits, vegetables, canned foods, cold cuts, soft drinks, and sundries that filled the front half of the store kept us stocked as a household. We would have had far less money if we had not been able to get our groceries at wholesale prices. But it was the quirky humanity that wandered into the rear half of the store that made us truly rich.

Even though there was always a panic every June when it came time to find the money to renew the beer license, we were wealthy in a way that is only now appreciated by me. The diversity of odd characters and the philosophies they brought with them into the City Market were an education that no Harvard boy ever got. So, in a rather rose-colored way, I am the product of a privileged upbringing.

My earliest memories of "the store", as we called it, were as a place that I would visit briefly with my grandfather. He was recovering from stomach surgery when I was four years old, and he was working limited hours at that point. He would watch me in the mornings, then take me with him to the store, and relieve my grandmother, who would return home with me for the afternoon. We went by taxi, and by bus a few times, and I can recall one day when he announced that we'd walk downtown. "I believe we'll walk today," he said, which was his invariable style in making a decision: *I believe* I'll walk. *I believe* I'll have something to eat.

It was a sunny, warm day, and I guess he had recovered enough of his stamina that it seemed like a good idea. I watched him finish dressing, buttoning up his white shirt and selecting a necktie from a bunch that dangled from hooks on the wall. He looked at me and said, "Wait a minute," and searched through the collection of ties until he found one that was shorter. He sat down, pulled me closer, and tied the short, wide, 1940s cravat around my neck. I beamed. I ran into the other bedroom and looked at myself in the vanity mirror. The tie still hung down below my waist, even though he had put a few extra turns in the knot, but I didn't care. I was wearing a tie, just like Grandpa, and I was ready to go out.

As we started down the sidewalk from the house, we encountered the elderly man who lived somewhere up the street. He was a disheveled old man who always wore a rumpled midnight blue wool suit with little white tick marks in the fabric. He smiled a mostly toothless smile and began waving as he approached. Grandpa said hello. The man looked at me and waved his hand enthusiastically, and said the same thing he always said when he saw me. "'Allo, Jimmy!" he said. He giggled slightly. Then a little softer, as he passed: "'Allo, Jimmy."

"Why don't you tell him your real name?" Grandpa said. I didn't know how to respond. I had once asked Grandma why the old man always called me "Jimmy", and she said only, "It was his son's name." The implication of the word "was", and her somber tone, was not lost on me, even at such a young age. It had the sound of Things Better Not Discussed, a tone I would become very familiar with during my growing up.

We walked down the street, past the hospital where Grandpa had his operation and where I could only wave to him from the parking lot, because only children over the age of 12 were allowed as visitors. He had come to the window to wave back to me while family members alternated visiting him and taking care of me, and now I looked up at that window and wondered who was in that room now. The air smelled of ether, as it often did, throughout the neighborhood around the hospital. Around the bend lay the downtown section of our city.

The streets were populated now, in mid-morning, and Grandpa spoke to various people we passed. We turned down Pleasant Street from the main street and things looked more familiar. As we approached the store, we stopped to talk to a man my family referred to as Bomb Butch. He was a tailor, and he was standing outside his shop, which was in the lower level under a clothing store. A pole jutted out from the sidewalk in front, with "Tailor" painted on it, and he had a measuring tape draped around his neck as though he had just been sizing someone up when the sidewalk called to him. He could often be seen standing outside the building, there on lower Pleasant Street. He and Grandpa talked briefly in Italian, then Bomb Butch went back inside. Then we arrived at the store, two doors down the street.

Grandma asked me what I had been doing that morning, and I said "Talking to Bomb Butch." She giggled. Everyone in the family would giggle when I said the name, a reaction I didn't understand, but would finally come to know as a compliment of sorts. I was pronouncing the man's name—Bomboccio—just as a native *Abbruzese* Italian would pronounce it. Bomb Butch.

At the age of fourteen, Grandpa had come from the province of Abruzzi in Italy to join his father, who had already immigrated to America. His father was a stonemason, and I later learned that the bricks of many of the streets I walked across in our town—those that were still brick—were laid by him. My great-grandfather Pietro Negri had left behind a wife and four children in "the old country" with hopes of prosperity here that apparently never materialized. He died in the late 1920s, having never returned to Italy nor securing passage for the rest of his family.

Grandpa worked as a young man, as did many other Italian immigrants, in the "tin mill"—the American Tin Plate Company plant (later to become Sterling Faucet Company). At the age of eighteen Bartolo Negri took as his wife thirteen year-old Edelina Alfieri, who was only too glad to escape a house of nine siblings and a stormy and violent father. She once told me, "It's a terrible thing to say, but I hated my father."

"Lena", as she was known, had already joined the work force at a printing company. She had a sixth-grade education. Grandpa went to the third grade. An amazingly different time.

Grandpa saved his money from the tin mill and invested in a venture that would make him self-employed. With a partner, he started a grocery-confectionary store that did well. Within a time, they opened a second store. Then the partnership soured and Grandpa ended up operating the second store independently. Later he and Grandma moved to a prime location in the heart of the central business district, at the corner of High and Pleasant Streets, and the boom years were on.

The City Market, as it was now called, had an entrance on the corner between two display windows that showed off the fruits, vegetables, and other staples that they sold. But there was another door on the High Street side that led more directly to the rear section of the room—the one that housed the tavern. Here, the local citizens of all callings stopped in for a beer on the way home, picking up a few groceries at the same time. Lawyers, doctors, and other professionals preferred to take their suds here, for it was more discreet to go into a grocery store than a saloon.

And the suds themselves had more to recommend them. Grandpa served the coldest beer in town. The cooler kept it at a lower temperature than anyone else was offering, and this popularized the tavern. Served up in frosty, fishbowl-like glasses, Grandpa's beer business was the backbone of the store, and his prosperity.

Decades later, I was talking with the owner of the most popular college beer-drinking establishment across town and he admitted to me that his inspiration for his beer temperature came from my grandfather. He never mentioned the fishbowl glasses, which had become his trademark.

Above: The original City Market exterior at the corner of High and Pleasant Streets.

Left: The side of the building looking down High St. The bar entrance to the City Market is in the center. The Warner Theater and the Hotel Morgan can be seen in the background.

For years, Grandpa and Grandma made a relatively secure living. They raised two daughters, Connie and Eleanor, who both achieved college degrees. Connie worked at various jobs and Eleanor got married and moved to the southern part of the state, having a child, Yours Truly. This coincided with a financial reversal all around.

Mom had been one of the top radio writers in the state when she had to quit the business to have me. Dad had to work both his radio announcing job and another job selling advertising in order to make ends meet. Tensions mounted. She left him, taking me and returning to her parents' home when I was eighteen months old.

The building that housed the City Market was condemned by the city at about the same time. It was the former home of a local historical figure, Colonel William McCleery, and was built in 1790. It became a commercial building after his time, as the town grew. It is unclear whether it had been neglected or was simply too old to remain, but it was soon torn down.

Grandpa moved the store to a vacant storefront two blocks down the side street, and that was the start of a slow death for the City Market. For some reason, even in a small town and even in a time when people walked often, a change of location to a side street could spell doom. People would not walk around the corner to the same store they had patronized for years. Besides this interesting facet of human psychology, there was another strike against the new location: Pleasant Street was Morgantown's "skid row".

The street was lined with legitimate businesses, to be sure; two men's shops (but not the *fine* men's shops), two furniture stores (but not the *good* furniture stores), two auto supply stores, a paint shop, an army surplus store. But the Salvation Army headquarters was across the street from our new location, which insured a number of less-than-prosperous citizens occupying the street every day. And there were several seedy taverns, a second-hand store called The Trading Post, a low-rent residential hotel without even a sign, and around the corner, the United Mineworker's Lodge, a bar which had nothing to do with a labor union and had prostitutes available upstairs.

Against this backdrop, I began my childhood. The comedown was particularly hard on my grandfather, who had not saved money and thought the gravy train was going to roll indefinitely. Now his unemployed daughter and a baby were under his roof and he must have felt a distinct panic, although he was never one to show it. He developed severe gastric ulcers, and believed he was going to die.

In those days of the early 1950s, the only conventional solution for his problem was surgery. But Grandpa had no health insurance, as few did in those times, and once Mom was again employed, she tried to use that status to try to guarantee a bank loan for the operation. She was repeatedly turned down. Finally one sympathetic bank officer approved the loan, and Grandpa had the surgery. They had to remove half his stomach. His paunch would grow back eventually, but my earliest memory of him is of a much thinner man than the one who would be around in my later childhood.

During his convalescence, he would look after me in the mornings, dress for going out (tightening his belt several notches further than before the surgery), and put a necktie on me so I felt like I belonged. Then we would leave the house and I would feel a thrill at the anticipation of slowly approaching the downtown district with all its sights, smells, buildings, and people. The walk downtown was part of Grandpa's path back to vitality, but now that I look back on it, it was just as important for me. I wasn't an active kid, and the walk likely helped balance the lack of typical childhood play and roughhousing that gave other children their strength and coordination.

So there we were, like two unsteady little kids walking slowly down the sidewalk to the family business, holding hands as we passed the very hospital without which I might never have had a grandfather growing up. I came to know all the little details of the route to the store. The places where someone had stuck his finger in the cement while it was still wet, atop the barriers that enclosed the hospital parking lot. The elevated curb surrounding the new VFW building, which I liked to balance on for a short distance. The shoe shine shop, which had a mannequin's leg sticking out of the side of the building, with a boot on it. The police call box, located high up on a telephone pole, which thrilled me one day when I saw the policeman there reach inside and pull out a telephone receiver. A telephone on a pole, outside!

One day as we were passing The Trading Post, the junk store on the corner above our store, I heard a funny voice. Looking up, I saw a bird in a cage on a shelf above the entrance. The bird was talking. We went closer to look at it.

It was black with a white spot on the side of its head. "That's a mynah bird," Grandpa said. "It can talk?" I asked. Just then the bird said, "What's your name?" I just stood there, transfixed.

In a strange replay of our encounter with the old man from up the street, Grandpa said, "Well, why don't you tell him your name?" I did. The bird replied, incredibly, "Ohhh, that's a nice name!"

Childhood memories are easy to distort, but I am still willing to swear (as I enter my seventh decade!) that that bird later called me by name every time it saw me. The two rough-looking men who sat on chairs outside the store would smile, amused. In thinking back on this, I am tempted to think that they were playing a joke, but there were times that the bird talked to me when no one was sitting there. Who knows?

3

One day I was staring out the front window of the City Market at the Salvation Army building across the street. I pronounced it "the salivation army", which made everyone giggle again and left me mystified. Didn't I say it just like they did?

But I was looking at it, by whatever name I knew it. It was a whitewashed 19th Century brick house with a walled-in courtyard in front. There were kids playing in the open section of the wall, which was used as a driveway, and one child was sitting atop the wall itself. Grandpa stood next to me, looked at the kids, and said, "Orphans." I'm not sure why he thought they were orphans, but for a number of years I thought that the salivation army was an orphanage. After a moment, he changed the subject. "Want to play the pinball machine? Let's go play the pinball machine."

The pinball machine was in the middle of the room between the far end of the bar and the last booth, crammed in to provide one more enticement for the patrons to linger and buy another beer, and I learned many years later that my family did as many in business in those days did: They paid off on winning games. This might be confusing to Twenty-first Century readers, but high scores on a pinball game entitled you to free plays, and people were more likely to sink more coins into the machine if something more than glory was the reward. The store received a percentage of the earnings of the machine every week when the man from the amusement company came to empty the coin vault. The take was always greater in establishments that made the hush-hush, illegal payoffs.

A small wooden stool sat under the machine, and Grandpa pulled it out for me to stand on, put a coin in the slot, and let me do my thing. I knew from practice to give the plunger a good pull back and to let it go quickly, insuring that the ball traveled with good speed. The bumpers chimed and lit up as the ball bounced rapidly back and forth and made its inevitable way down to the hole. As I was looking up at the scoreboard, I felt hands around my ribs, and my grandmother snatched me off the stool and practically levitated me through the curtains into the back room.

A policeman had come into the front part of the store. While Grandpa waited on him, Grandma explained to me that it was against the law for minors to play pinball. I must have started to protest, because she said "Do you want us to get arrested?!" We went back out front and the patrolman was still there. He glanced at me. He was hard looking.

Grandma got a half pint of chocolate milk for me (always with two paper straws) and gave me a seat in the first booth.

I was appeased by the chocolate milk but sat there wondering why coal miners couldn't play pinball and what it had to do with me. Against the law for miners?

I lingered there for a time after finishing my milk until Grandma told me I had to leave the booth. Flossie was here. Flossie always sat where I was now sitting. She was a jowly little woman who didn't smile; a scrubwoman, I believe. She always wore a scarf over her head and tied under her chin, which made her sagging cheeks poke out like a soft stuffed doll. She would drink her Black Label beer ("a lady's beer," Grandma told me often) and sit facing the front and not interact with anyone. There wasn't anything to see by facing front in the first booth—only the meat slicer and ice cream freezer. But she wasn't interested in the television or the other people or anything. Her saggy, sad face was fixed on the bottle of beer in front of her whenever she occupied the space. The first booth was Flossie's. I don't recall anyone else ever preferring a particular booth.

Why is Black Label for "ladies"? I put the question to Grandma once. "Oh, it's *sweet*." Grandpa gave me a taste of it and I wouldn't have categorized it as even *near* sweet. Chocolate milk, that's sweet. But the thrill of tasting beer had its own attraction, no matter what the stuff tasted like.

Another regular came in the store as I waited for my mother to come get me. Jay the Midget strolled in and hopped on the ornate iron stool that stood at the head of the bar. All the other barstools were upholstered, some with seat backs, but this one had a plain wooden seat and was actually a survivor of an ice cream parlor in the early 1900s. How it ended up in the City Market I never learned, but Jay the Midget always sat there, perhaps because it made him look taller, or he just didn't have to turn his head to see the television, since the set was mounted on a shelf in the rear that looked straight down the bar toward that spot.

Television. It was not a rarity at that point in time, but still not yet an omnipresent piece of living room *accoutrements*, at least for the locals in my community. For a place like the City Market, it was still a good business strategy to advertise (as we did on our front window) that the place had television. And Jay the Midget watched with rapt attention, no matter what appeared on the fuzzy screen.

Thinking back, Jay the Midget was not a dwarf; he had a slight bow-legged gait but his limbs were not short. He was proportionate; maybe technically what everyone called a midget in those days. Or just a *little guy*. But he was known as Jay the Midget. He always wore a plaid cloth cap and I never saw him take it off. Grandpa saluted him with a "Hiya, Jay," and put a beer in front of him as the skinny little guy pulled out his cigarettes and settled in for an hour or so.

I wouldn't be there to see him leave. Mom came to pick up Grandpa and me, and home we went for dinner. Grandpa would eat with the two of us, then take a nap before going back to the store until closing. These would not necessarily be communal meals in that typical-family sense; there might be a little conversation, but not much. This pattern would persist all through my growing up. Grandpa would eat quickly, looking for that nap to come; I came to do likewise, to shorten my time at the kitchen table where I would have to endure arguments, mostly between my mother and Connie.

Jay the Midget

My mother's sister, four years her senior, was an oddity. She had one characteristic that overpowered all others and defined her: She was argumentative. It was not the uncomplicated quality that could be found in thousands of Italian family homes, with people yelling, gesticulating wildly, and seemingly at each other's throats as a form of cultural expression. Connie just picked fights, free of ethnicity (and often free of logic). She lacked maturity for some reason, and frequently expressed sentiments that were juvenile. Today, with psychology more developed as a science than in those days, her condition is defined as a "personality disorder". But it mattered little whether it was an illness (as seen today) or just a "disagreeable nature"— Connie would make my growing up in that house... challenging.

Because of her essential immaturity, it was like growing up with another sibling, an older one who bullied you. I had a few chances to hear, over the years, of the fights my friends would have with their brothers. The fact that I had to face many of the same trials, in spite of being an only child, and *with my mother's older sister*, no less, was exasperating to me. Like other kids who have to endure their siblings tormenting them when their parents weren't around, or running to Mom first and blaming the younger kid for something they did, I had to endure Connie doing all the same things regardless of the fact that she was a fully grown adult. I suppose my appearance on the scene aroused her jealousy from the very start; lots of attention was lavished on the grandchild in that house. To someone with an adolescent personality, that could invoke some real resentment.

One of her early displays was particularly cruel, and illustrates the situation. Connie and I were alone in the living room one morning. I think she was between jobs, which was the case throughout a good bit of my childhood, and that made her available to watch me. I was around five years old. On that day, she pretended to die. She collapsed on the couch, eyes closed, and did not respond when I called her. "Aunt Connie, Aunt Connie," I was crying. Her arm dangled off the edge and I pulled on her hand. It was floppy and lifeless. I stood in the center of the room and began crying harder. Then she sat up and laughed at me. She mocked me, copying my tearful words: "Wah! Aunt Connie, Aunt Connie…" She said it in a blubbering voice and then laughed at me again. I was stunned. I had no indignation, only shock. I had never before been deceived, nor humiliated. I had no idea what I was supposed to think.

Some months passed, and we were in the living room alone again. She was drinking something and choked on it. After coughing for a minute, she "expired" on the couch again. "Aunt Connie?" I inquired, a little more wary this time. She didn't move. I waited a minute, and then ran to the telephone in the hall. By this time, you see, I had learned the phone number of the City Market.

By the time I had dialed half of the number in order to reach my grandmother, Connie suddenly revived. "Wait!" she cried. "I'm okay!" I stood looking at her from the hall. "What happened? I remember choking…" she said. I didn't have the vocabulary to say or even think "You won't bullshit me again," but that was the sentiment that formed that day. And just then, my grandfather descended the stairs, asking what I was doing with the telephone, and I began telling him. Connie started talking rapidly, telling him that we were playing, and I saw him give her an incisive look I had never seen before. I had the City Market's number, but Grandpa had Connie's number. It would be many years later that I would learn just how Grandpa had her figured out, and that her behavior had never really been any different.

Connie gets chummy with a City Marketeer.

4

Christmas time, even on Pleasant Street, was exciting. The city put up decorations on the telephone poles; not as grand as those on the more main streets, but they certainly added color to an otherwise run-down few blocks. We sprayed "snow" that came in aerosol cans onto the windows of the store, through cardboard stencils that made the shapes of bells, and holly leaves, and one that spelled out "Merry Christmas".

Very exciting was the view, from the sidewalk in front of the store, of Jerry's Auto Supply. One wouldn't think a kid would have any fondness for a place like that, but this time of year the lower part of the neon sign that hung on the front of the building had a special appeal. It was the part that said, in red neon, TOYS. For some reason, Jerry's was also a toy store. After you passed the aisles with the oil filters, batteries, and miscellaneous cranks, levers, and tools (one could only guess some of their uses), there were a couple aisles that had toys crammed on the shelves in the same way as the other merchandise. Jerry's was a slightly confusing place for me as a kid, because I couldn't seem to square the loud-talking men and cigar smoke with fun things, as found on the toy counters of other stores like Murphy's and Woolworth's. But Jerry's had their version of a kid's emporium, although they carried the kind of toys that the children of men who tinkered with cars played with: erector sets, model cars, toy versions of hunting and fishing gear, etc. Once I had a chance to survey the stock, I wasn't as excited.

But I had stopped in there with Mom, who chatted with the men behind the counter that day. All the merchants on

Pleasant Street knew each other, and Mom was talking with one guy I had seen in our store, named Ted. He had a cigar in the corner of his mouth, and a hot water bottle stuffed in the rear of his trousers waistband. My mother inquired. "Muscle spasm," he said, mouthing the words with a little difficulty around the fat cylinder in his mouth. I understood the word "muscle", but the other one sounded like "spazzum", which I was sure couldn't be a real word and decided I misunderstood him. Still, it wasn't important enough to ask about it afterward, because we were going next door to Hav-A-Lunch. Yay!

Hav-A-Lunch was a wonderful example of a downtown diner that exists in few places today, and *everyone* in town ate there. There was only counter service. Two semi-circular counters with stools filled the place, and there was a huge stainless steel coffee urn to one side. Huge! Waitresses were mostly older women, career servers who had regular customers and treated them right. Their slogan, painted on the sign, was "No Beer, Just Good Food". Charmingly funny, now.

Mom and I entered, found a couple empty wall hooks to hang our coats, and grabbed two vacant stools. I knew what I wanted. Pancakes. I loved their pancakes, and I couldn't figure out what was different about them but I knew that they never had the slightly scorched underside that the ones made at home had. I probably made my mother feel deflated about preferring commercial pancakes, but I couldn't stand that tough, lacey edge that hers always had (a defect that sometimes marred the eggs, too). Here the edges of the cakes were smooth, the maple syrup plentiful, and I was in heaven.

It wasn't just the stack of flapjacks that made being there a treat. The restaurant itself was a bit of big city that I observed in movies and TV shows, and made me believe (for a while, at least) that my town was no different from the metropolitan locales of the shows I watched. Hav-A-Lunch even had a mural of New York harbor on the back wall of the place. I loved gazing at the rows of boat docks and the steamships in the harbor, the skyscrapers towering above them. The crowded humanity on the stools, many of whom I would come to recognize as prominent downtowners, created an atmosphere that I found exciting. Pleasant Street was my neighborhood, my turf.

That Christmas, I received a present from one of the City Market regulars, Al Flenniken. Al gave me a cowboy gun belt, a broad, honey-colored leather belt with two holsters. I had a couple holsters and six-shooters already (although single holsters—could shoot only half as many bad guys), so it was not a crushing disappointment to find that it was too big for me. "He'll grow into it" is a phrase every kid becomes used to. But it ignited a creativity that I would hone to a fine edge as I aged. As I would do with many things in the coming years, I simply made it into something else.

I had a stuffed horse, a pillow made to look like a horse that you sat on and "rode". I took the oversized gun belt and made it into a saddle for my horse. I sat on the wide leather back of the belt, and slipped my feet into the holsters that hung over the sides, using them as stirrups. It just about worked. Mom seemed impressed with my ingenuity. Now my cowboy ensemble was more authentic than ever, and in that time period, when there were more than a dozen western TV shows on the air, that was important.

Al was a good-natured guy who sat at the bar often and knew all the other regulars. One time I noticed a bluish design peeking up from behind the top of his unbuttoned shirt. I asked him what it was. "You wanna see that, kid?" he asked. He unbuttoned the shirt down to his waist and pulled it open. He had an eagle tattooed across his entire chest. The others grinned as they watched my face register bewilderment. I'd seen tattoos before, but never anything like this. It was the American eagle, right off a dollar bill or coin or some other patriotic item.

Connie was there that day helping out, and maybe Al was partly motivated to bare his chest in order to get a reaction from her. Remembering it now, Connie was as flirty with certain customers as she was unfriendly to all the rest; Al was certainly one of the people my family members felt close to.

Another customer entered the front of the store and Connie walked over to wait on him. It was Cocky John. "Hi, Cocky," she said pleasantly to the most bizarrely shaped man I had ever seen in my short life. He had a huge abdomen that protruded an incredible distance in front of him yet he was not all that fat anywhere else. He always wore just a white undershirt that stretched across this vast expanse, which remained nevertheless neatly tucked into his waistband. I had to stare at his girth, if for no reason other than it was eye level for me, and I noticed that the belt that looped around these huge trousers had still some reserve. A long end emerging from the buckle dangled down from the next belt loop and hung in front of the pleats on the left side. I wondered what the longest belt available was.

Cocky had come for the same item I always saw him buy: a box of Fig Newtons. He made small talk with Connie as she rang up the sale, and he wasted no time opening the package and starting to devour some of the cookies. I was intimidated by the grotesque sight of Cocky somehow; he walked with an unhurried, deliberate gait and the sight of that stomach slowly moving toward me seemed threatening, like an ocean liner headed right for your little fishing boat. I could imagine being capsized on dry land by that gut!

After Cocky left, Connie asked if I wanted a Fig Newton. I declined. Watching Cocky chew them might have been enough to sour me on the idea, but I had tried them once and didn't like the texture of the little gritty fig seeds inside. Grandma said figs had a lot of iron, and I concluded that what I was crunching on were little bits of iron. I didn't know until I was much older that figs had seeds, which coincided with the time I found out what figs *were*.

I decided on Vanilla Wafers instead, and Connie opened a box. They were tasty, and safe. No surprises inside.

I must have started to get in the way there in the store, because I was told to go say hello to the folks next door. Our neighbor to the west was Fox Auto Supply, owned by longtime customer Bill Fox. Bill and all his employees frequented our store, and they were part of the extended family of Pleasant Street. Bill had started with one storefront and had expanded to three, one of which sold appliances like refrigerators and washing machines. I went into the appliance entrance and everyone was busy. So I walked farther down the street to visit someplace I liked more—a men's clothing store called Weintrob's.

Max Weintrob was a rail-thin, elderly tailor with wire-rim glasses, thin gray hair, and a classic Jewish affect. He was in business with his nephew Seymour, a man with a thin moustache and a suit that seemed to fit him better than Max's. Another man worked there, named Mr. Walker. It is interesting to me now, how I was taught to call the others Max and Seymour, even though I was a little kid; yet Mr. Walker was always *Mister Walker*, even when addressed by my mother.

So there I was, paying a visit to my friends in the haberdashery, and they welcomed me as they might have any adult friend. I chatted with each one in turn, and when one had to tend to a customer, another would take his place. I mentioned that I was hoping to hide from Aunt Connie, and Seymour took me through a doorway. I actually got to see the back room for the first time, where there was a sewing machine and steam press and a large table with measuring marks along the edges. It was magical. Seymour placed me on a platform and told me that he was drawing "invisible" curtains around me and that nobody could see me if I stayed right there—a clever ploy that allowed them to get some work done.

After a bit, I was taken back out front and old Max asked me with a smile, "So do you think your Aunt Connie is crabby?" The other men chuckled. I grinned. I had never heard the word "crabby", and it sounded very humorous. I said, "Yes." They all laughed audibly then.

A moment later, Connie came in the door, having searched for me at each storefront down the street. "Come on, let's go," she said, as she walked back to the fitting area where we were. Still giggling from hearing the new word, I told her "He said you're *crabby*. Hee hee!"

The three men turned abruptly and went in different directions. "There's somebody up front," said Mr. Walker as he raced to the counter. Seymour picked something up and carried it into the back room. I was looking at Connie and saw her eyebrow arch, the corner of her mouth turn down, saw her face form the scowl that was her trademark. She grabbed my hand and led me out. Crabby, indeed.

5

As I advanced through grade school, I would bring friends of mine to the store from time to time. On one such day, I brought my friend Skipper with me, and Grandpa made ice cream sodas for the two of us. Grandpa was evidently pleased with my impromptu visit in the afternoon; he was very affectionate and later Skipper commented on it. "Gee, he sure likes you!" was his observation.

Yes, he liked me, and since I was getting older and not seeing him as much as before I was in school, I suppose that made our little interludes that much more special. In the little kitchen in the back of the store, he would grate Romano cheese while I watched and I would sample the overflow as it was put into a large mason jar. The table was covered with a "tablecloth" of newspaper, which was changed every so often. I would sweep the little curly bits of cheese with the edge of my hand, and after eating them, notice ink on my hand. Grandpa would make salads that were delicious, even to a kid who didn't get excited about salads. Wine vinegar, olive oil, garlic, and anchovies mixed with the lettuce, tomatoes and red onions in a medley that couldn't be beat. My mouth waters today at the thought of it. There was always enough of the delectable dressing left in your bowl that you could dip some crusty Italian bread in it afterward, and that was the best part. A few little bits of anchovy clinging to the bread were a taste sensation that I had no idea so few Americans enjoyed.

That makeshift kitchen at the City Market was sectioned off by curtains that separated it from the rest of the back room. Outside that curtained perimeter, empty bottles were stacked in wooden boxes, a year's supply of paper bags topped a wide table, and in the corner, a long wooden flagpole with an impossibly dusty flag rolled up on it. The pole was about 12 feet long, and I had asked about it and was told that it used to be put out in a hole in the sidewalk on national holidays. I wondered where that hole was. Evidently it had been in front of the old store, before the move to Pleasant Street.

On the other side of the back room were the two rest rooms, like little sheds with their own flat roofs inside the larger room. The tin ceilings at the store were perhaps twenty feet high. The rest rooms had been retro-fitted into the space and were…well, the kind of place that beer-drinking men with tattoos felt at home peeing in. When I was very young, the men's room only had a trough-style urinal; health codes must have dictated the toilet that was installed later. An old wall-mounted sink with separate taps was hanging around the corner, outside the rest rooms.

But the City Market kitchen, tucked away behind the curtains, saw a lot of delectables prepared there on a little two-burner gas tabletop stove and another small kitchen range beside it. Customers would bring in fresh game sometimes and Grandpa would prepare it. Grandma made pizza twice a week in the oven back there, also. Slices were wrapped in wax paper and sold at the bar for fifteen cents. The kitchen was hidden from view, not simply because it was private, but because we did not have a restaurant license. I can only imagine what it would have cost to comply with the health code.

My favorite part of the back room, though, was the partition that separated it from the rest of the store. More specifically, a dark area that contained a small table flanked by coat hooks, with a storage shelf above it. Our coats hung to the right of the table, and a supply of aprons hung on the left. Some boxes stacked on the shelf above shadowed the already dim light so that the table against the wall was barely visible. On the table was a brass banker's lamp, only used for a minute at a time. Here Grandma would write checks for the deliverymen when an order came in. But none of this is really what attracted me. Above the table, cut into the wall was a peephole. One could look out and see who was in the store, all the way to the front door. The people at the bar would appear to be looking right at you, but the television set on the shelf above the hole was what they were really looking at.

What a wonderfully sneaky, appealing thing for a kid!

I don't know what prompted the peephole having been cut into that wall, since there were no card games in the back room or anything else that I could imagine my grandparents wanting to be on guard over. But I did slowly catch on to the fact that there were harmless practices at the City Market that were not strictly legal. The home-cooked pizza was not a major example. The pinball machine was done away with by the time I was seven or eight, so that was no longer there to attract attention from passing policemen.

But two things were constant through the years that, once I understood them, I had to be quiet about. The first was "playing the numbers". Young people today are not aware that before state government sponsored daily lotteries, people bet—illegally—in what was known as the "numbers racket". The numbers in question were derived daily from the closing points of the New York Stock Exchange. By what formula this was done, I don't recall, but it resulted in a three-digit number and that is what people tried to guess. Betting a dollar on 123 "straight" means you only won if that exact number came out; but if you bet 123 "boxed" you could win for 123, 132, 213, 231, 312, or 321. However, since the odds are less against you with this 6-way chance, you win less money than if you made a "straight" bet.

Supposedly, the numbers racket was an Italian invention. But the American public in every city was very familiar with "bookies" who placed your bets for you, and "runners" who carried the money in both directions. In the case of the City Market, it was very easy to place bets because of Albert. He worked next door at the Army-Navy surplus store, came in our store multiple times daily, and was known to most of the men by his nickname, "Ike". No one in my family ever called him anything but Albert, though. He would come in, converse with my grandmother, take out a little piece of paper and write something with a pencil. The paper would go back into his pocket and he would be off.

Grandma believed in the significance of dreams; not in the Freudian sense, but in a mystical way. She had a number of "dream books" that told you what a particular dream subject meant—you looked them up alphabetically (A tip: Dreaming of poop is lucky!). She consulted these books often, and I finally noticed that under each heading there was a three-digit number. She played the number of her dream content, and often won.

The second questionable enterprise that my family was involved with was the "pool" where people bet on the final score of an upcoming ball game. There were two types, small and big. The small ones only accommodated ten or so people. The big ones, which I liked because they involved art, had a hundred chances to win. I helped out on these projects, drawing the board on the back of a page torn off from the calendar. I would draw a grid of a hundred squares and Grandma would tear little strips of paper and write the numbers 0 to 9 on them. Drawing them out of a hat one by one, the numbers were written across the top in whatever order they cam out and then the slips were drawn again and written down one side of the grid. The columns were for the home team and the rows were for the opposing team. The idea was that you chose a particular square, paid a quarter, and signed your name inside the square. If your square happened to be the intersection of the column 9 and row 2, the final score of the game would have to be 19-12 (for example) for you to win. The numbers were covered until all the squares had been sold, so this was really a game of chance.

My personal financial life began when I was twelve and took the last two chances on a football pool. It was a Saturday afternoon, a big game everyone was excited about (I couldn't have cared less), and a memorable day because I won the pool! Everyone was amused that the kid won, and I received $22.50 that evening for my luck. The next week, I went to the First National Bank up the street by myself and opened my first checking account. It cost me one dollar for the checkbook.

If the numbers racket seems archaic, the idea of opening a bank account with no fees beyond a dollar, and no identification, by a twelve year-old—well, that *really* makes you feel like you've lived a long time.

Another thing that happened that seems as if from another age was when the gypsies would come into town in the spring. Real, honest-to-gosh gypsies, looking just like they do in the movies: heavy makeup, lots of bangles, dangling earrings, flowing skirts with wide leather belts. They came in our store a couple times and Grandma was uncharacteristically short with them—*Buy something or get out.* The three women had separated, looking at the produce, the tinned meats, and the third lingering around the cash register. Grandma planted herself in front of the register, and gave them another thirty seconds of their indefinite wandering, and then ordered them out.

This would have been seen to be a prejudicial thing if not for the fact that the next day, newspapers carried the story that multiple businesses downtown had been robbed by gypsies, who had a method of distracting store personnel while pocketing goods and, in one instance, rifling the cash register. This happened yearly, and police learned to be on alert for them around Easter time. Grandma apparently did not have to rely on police intelligence to be on her guard. They were gypsies, and she knew what they were up to.

On that occasion, and many others, I was anxious over the confrontation. I was always scared to watch Grandma throw people out of the City Market, worried at even a young age about retaliation or on-the-spot violence. Yet she was always successful, even when met with some resistance— when a drunk did not vacate soon enough—and she nudged him along with a firm grasp on the offender's shirt collar and the seat of his pants. With his pants jacked up and his collar pulled back, the drunk was forced up on his toes and moved swiftly along to the door with Grandma's locomotion. She had been doing this a long time, but it always made me nervous.

The most frightening of all was one time when she threw out the man I called "Voo Tavoo". Voo Tavoo was the biggest, scariest man I had ever seen. There were a couple other scary characters who were regulars, too, but none as visually menacing as Voo Tavoo. He was a large man, over six feet tall, broad-shouldered and unkempt. His baggy pants were dirty and his suit coat rumpled and moth-eaten. He wore a floppy hat that retained none of its original shape, and hair protruded here and there from underneath. He always had a several-day growth of beard, very dark hair that looked prickly like thorns on a cactus. His eyes were black, not just dark. And his distinguishing characteristic was his upper lip, which was cleft deeply and the two sides bulged at different angles, and bristled with spiky black stubble. Presumably, it was impossible to shave in the deep groove, scar, or whatever it was, because it was filled with more of the black hair, and the scar was made all the more obvious because of it. He was a hard man to look at. He was a hard man, period.

He worked on the city street crew. I saw him on occasion, riding in the old city truck with wooden sideboards on the bed and a pick, shovel, and broom attached to the wood. Voo Tavoo would sometimes ride in the bed or stand on the rear bumper, hanging onto the sideboard casually as though there wasn't a danger in the world. He came in the store once in a while, and on this evening that I happened to be there he was sitting in a booth with three other people drinking beer.

I have no idea whether anyone truly understood anything Voo Tavoo said; I sure didn't. Ordering a beer was easy to figure out, so I don't know to what extent my grandmother or grandfather understood the speech of this big man with a cleft palate. But it wasn't as though he made a lot of conversation.

That evening, something in the discussion at that table angered Voo Tavoo, because his voice got loud. I don't remember if I heard any of the argument, but the big man got to his feet, pointed his finger at the man who was sitting opposite him, and said "Voo tavoo!" The other man started to speak again and the voice of the big man boomed. "Voo ta VOO!" He stood there defiantly, his legs spread as if ready for action, his finger still pointing to the other man when Grandma came around the bar and said, "That's enough! You get out now!" He glowered at the occupants of the booth, hesitated for a moment during which my body stiffened and my lungs forgot to breathe, and then turned and left the store. I was immensely thankful that the incident did not turn into a bloody melee. I was a big worrier for a kid.

From that day on, the nameless man with the scary visage was known to me as Voo Tavoo, based on this unintelligible epithet he had hurled. My friends, whom I told the story, referred to him as Voo Tavoo also.

It was not until I was in my twenties that I revisited my memory of Voo Tavoo and realized that the man had likely been shouting "F*ck you!"

Voo Tavoo

6

The man who probably got thrown out of the City Market more often than anyone else was "Mac" MacMillen. He was a comical-looking skinny old man that my grandmother nicknamed "Andy Gump" for his resemblance to a comic strip character from the 1920s. He was practically chinless, and his angular face seemed to just taper down to his pencil neck, from which protruded a prominent Adam's apple. Mac would sit in a booth by himself, drinking beer after beer, the number of which increased his interaction with the other drinkers. He would flit back and forth between his booth and the other booths or the bar, injecting himself into their conversations and prompting an outburst from Grandma. "Stop bothering people! Go back and drink your beer or get out!" Mac would walk back to his seat in little spurts, chuckling; something about drinking made him walk haltingly. He would enter the store with normal movements, bordering on the agile. He might have been a dancer, once. He always left with a slow, erratic gait. He reminded me of a crab, the way he would move slowly sideways, inching his way from person to person at the bar, making comments to each of them over their shoulders before finally being ordered to leave. I found him hugely entertaining.

I never got the impression that any of the other customers were actually bothered by him, but his often-nonsensical ramblings must have been resented by some. He was supremely irritating to Connie, however, which is probably why I liked him so much. It was amusing to watch her dramatize her annoyance with him, which she did to create a picture of a long-suffering persona in front of the customers. None of them really bought it. Scowling, clucking her tongue, folding her arms across her chest—she was *onstage* when she worked at the City Market, and Mac was her foil. He seemed to enjoy the fact that he got under Connie's skin, and would wander from his booth to her post and deliver some giggling monologue that an exasperated Connie would finally cut short with an order to go away. He would look at me and giggle some more. He was such a cartoonish figure I had to like him.

I never saw Grandpa throw Mac out. My grandfather was an amazingly tolerant man with a *laissez-faire* attitude in most things. I do recall him reining Mac in on one occasion, when he was bothering Ray Utt. Ray was having a beer at his customary #1 stool and Mac was hovering at his side, mumbling something. Ray looked annoyed and Grandpa said, "Hey!" That was all Mac needed. He went back to his seat.

When I say Ray looked annoyed, it has to be considered in light of the fact that Ray *always* looked annoyed. He was a plumber with a bad leg that caused him constant pain, which was obvious. He always limped in slowly, and settling his bulk into the barstool was done cautiously. I don't know what his problem was, but he did say one time "I'll never let them take my leg off!" So it was evidently serious enough that amputation was considered. Ray was a fleshy guy all over, but he carried most of his weight in his hips and thighs, like some women. When he walked, he planted his left foot and then swung the right leg slowly forward, with the knee bent and never straightening. It had a rhythm rather like a camel's walk, with his upper body inclining, then straightening. When he climbed up onto the barstool, you got a view of the biggest, roundest backside ever to frequent the City Market. He always wore denim overalls that stretched tightly over his bulk and there was always a wooden fold-up yardstick tucked in a narrow pocket that was made for it, in the work clothes of those days. His round face only showed its age around the eyes. Even when unshaven, it had a childlike quality. Sometimes he would make a certain expression and a large dimple appeared in his cheek. There was something cute about him, even though he always appeared to be pissed off.

Ray lived in a decaying building across the street that had been a hotel at one time. Now it was a low-rent residential building where workingmen (and some who *rarely* worked) had single rooms. About this time, a competing tavern opened up on the first floor of that building, the Sportsman's Bar. It was never mentioned by anyone in my family except in the context of who was staggering down the street after having been in there. As if no one ever staggered out of the City Market! But the selling of groceries seemed to give us a moral edge. The Sportsman's Bar was just a bar. In fact, the owner often came into our place to drink beer while someone else ran his place. He had a head of thick black hair combed back in a pompadour and looked very much like Johnny Cash.

In time, another challenger appeared on the next block. I noticed while walking down Pleasant Street to the store one day that a sign had been nailed to the outside of a storefront near Jerry's Auto Supply. It was a new place called the El Toro. The sign advertised in large letters "Big 10¢ Draft"! I conveyed this information to Grandpa, who responded with his customary "Huh?" No matter what I said, his first response was "Huh?" I would then repeat the information in the same tone and volume and he would hear it just fine. It was a little ritual that he indulged in, and I never believed his hearing was truly bad as the rest of my family members thought.

I took the news to Grandma also. "They're selling beer for ten cents!" This was at a time when a City Market draft was twenty-five cents. I wondered if they would undercut our business. Grandma just shook her head and smiled that smile that said she was tolerating something that didn't deserve comment. I felt (as I often did) slighted that no one valued what I had to say. I later walked up the street to sneak a look in the El Toro to see if they were succeeding in this cutthroat competition. Crossing the street to peer into the window, I realized that the sign actually said "Big 10 oz. Draft". The "ounce" abbreviation had been stylishly rendered so that it looked like a cent sign from a distance. I felt embarrassed over my premature reporting to my grandparents but then that gave way to a sort of admiration for the clever way the El Toro owners got people in the door, if it was deliberate. I still think it was.

I went back to the store to report my findings but Grandma just walked away while I was talking, to draw a beer for a customer. Seeing an opening, Hugh Runner engaged me in conversation because, well, nobody was listening to him either. Hugh talked in a loud, oratorical voice that made him seem like a politician. I think that is what he would have liked to have been. He sold insurance and real estate, and had an office in the Monongahela Building a block away. He was sixty or so, always wore a three-piece suit, and preferred the old wooden-seated stool at the head of the bar when it was not occupied by Jay the Midget. He liked to talk about the news of the day and world events, but his discussions rarely penetrated beyond the seat next to him. He was a little too intellectual for the City Market, I now realize. Other patrons would direct their attention to the TV set.

Grandpa stood behind the bar facing the screen also, with his hands behind his back as always. He seemed to hear the television just fine. I decided that his hard-of-hearing tendency was not an act but an unconscious coping device from having to live with three women in the same house who were perpetually arguing about something. Then Grandma said, "Buddy! Eleanor's here." "Buddy" was my grandmother's nickname for him. It was the only thing I ever heard her call him. Grandpa turned to look toward the street as I did, saw Mom in the car double-parked outside, and took off his apron. He hung it on the hook in the back room near the peephole, retrieved his hat from another hook, and we left for home and dinner.

Mom's arm was out the car window, making circular motions to indicate to the other drivers that they should go around her. Some did this only grudgingly; one car honked its horn as it passed. Mom made a disapproving sound. I jumped into the back seat, as was our ritual, while Grandpa repeated the somewhat mechanical process of taking his place in the passenger seat. I say that it was mechanical because he had a certain way of negotiating the door and the car seat, a method that became more pronounced as he aged. Both because he was stiffening from arthritis and gout and because the new cars (like our 1960 Chevrolet) had lower roofs than the old cars, there was a peculiar thing that would happen that amused me. He would open the door, turn around and sit down on the edge of the seat, and then get his left leg in while beginning to turn his body around to face front. During this process, his hat would catch the top of the car and flip forward off his head. He came to expect this, I guess, because he would place his hands in front of him, poised to receive the falling fedora. The hat would arrive, he would finish the turn, and he would put the hat back on his head and shut the door. This was repeated every time he entered the car.

I watched this process as a sort of entertainment, but it also came to take on a certain ritualistic quality. I don't recall ever worrying about what would happen if this little bit of awkwardness-turned-into-agility was omitted, but it was in some way a comfort that this funny thing was predictable. Increasingly, life would not be predictable. And, though I could not yet articulate it, these simple human actions gave me a sense that they were precious, even if mundane.

Back home, I shoveled my dinner into my mouth as fast as I could, which was my wont in those days, and then left to visit my best friend Ralph down the street. Grandpa always took a nap after dinner before returning to the store and, this being summer, liked to take it outside on the porch glider. This was a source of entertainment for Ralph and myself. We would sneak around the side of the porch and peer over the railing to look down at Grandpa sleeping. He always put one hand behind his head during these naps, sleeping on his back. A predictable thing would happen. As his sleep deepened, his breathing would change. He would draw a breath, then he would slowly exhale from the mouth. But his lips and then his cheeks would inflate before the air would finally escape with a "Poof!" sound, and then the cycle would repeat. It was like watching a pot of thick soup as it comes to a boil, slowly expanding until it divests itself of the air trapped within it. Ralph and I would stifle our laughter so as not to wake him up, and watch the process a few more times before it would progress to full-out snoring. It was the early-stage sleep that was most amusing, and we would walk back down the street to Ralph's house and sit on the stoop, mimicking the "Poof" sound.

Now, at the age of seventy, I wake myself up with the same sound if I chance to fall asleep on my back. I guess we never get too far from where we came from.

Later that evening, after Mom had chauffeured Grandpa home from the store, she asked if I wanted to go with her to pick Grandma from Bingo. It was her Bingo night, or one of them. She attended games at several locations whenever she could, and I knew she really enjoyed it. I said sure, I would go.

This night's activities were at the Sons of Italy lodge. "I thought we were going to the Turn Verein Hall," I said. "No," she corrected me, "they don't have them there anymore." I was slightly disappointed. I liked the neighborhood of that place.

The Sons of Italy was down a steep brick road below the Walnut Street Bridge, which loomed above. Now I was no longer disappointed. The moody, dimly lighted surroundings had the qualities of the mystery and suspense movies I watched on Saturday nights. It looked just like you might find an opium den in the basement of one of these buildings, or Bela Lugosi's henchman would step out of the shadows to grab some 1940s blonde and bring her to Bela's lab. Women were pouring out of the main doors and descending the concrete steps to the street. Grandma appeared, opened the door, and said, "Mrs. Slaven needs a ride home." The two women seated themselves in the back of the car, and I turned around to converse with the visitor. I hadn't seen Mrs. Slaven for a while. She asked all the usual questions: *How old are you now? What grade are you in? What do you like to do?*

Mom piloted the car to Pleasant Street. It seemed strange to be in the right lane, since our store was on the left side, but Mrs. Slaven lived above Jerry's Auto. We pulled up to the curb, and I got out to help Mrs. Slaven out of the car. She steadied herself on her cane, and made her way to the entrance, and I held the door for her. She thanked me, and as she started up the stairs, I saw something I never saw before. On the fifth or sixth step, there was a sign painted on the riser: Slaven Apartments.

"Gee, Mrs. Slaven owns the building?" I asked.

"Yes. Her son has the jewelry store." I knew where Slaven's Jewelry was, just a couple blocks away, but somehow I never connected it. While I was thinking about this, Grandma told Mom "Fleck can't come to bingo anymore. She's gotten too bad." "Fleck?" I asked. "Mrs. Fleckenstein," Mom whispered. "She's old and sick."

How can you be too old or sick to play bingo? I thought. I had only seen Mrs. Fleckenstein once, and it had been some time. I couldn't picture her clearly. I remembered that she had a lot of brown spots on her skin. As I thought about it she began to take on a monsterish look in my mind's eye. Flecks on the skin. Mrs. Fleckenstein. Mrs. *Frankenstein*. I snickered to myself. Mrs. Frankenstein playing bingo. Chuckle chuckle.

"What's so funny?" Mom said, sharply.

"Nothing."

7

There he was.   The man with the raincoat exiting the airplane and descending the steps to the tarmac was my father. I watched him cross to the gate; I watched alongside Mom and Grandma and Grandpa Lamb, his parents.   We watched, on the other side of the chain link fence, the man whom I vaguely remembered as one-third of my family… back in the beginning…

For some reason, my memory has always been more or less intact since early childhood. And I remembered, as I stood there on the day that my father returned to his hometown for a visit—I remembered the man who picked me up as a toddler, smiling, *beaming*, in fact, at me as I smiled at him. But it was a long time ago.

In spite of the fact that I remembered my father, his presence now made me feel uneasy. Regardless of the fact that there were no unpleasant associations with him, he was not part of my life, as I knew it. He was foreign.

Just as his parents were familiar but yet at the same time not part of the life I knew. In spite of the divorce, Mom saw to it that Dad's family was part of my life. But whenever I visited the Lamb family house, all the sights and sounds and smells were different. There was modular furniture in the living room, and paintings on the walls, and the aroma of cherry pipe tobacco in the air. There was a leather armchair and shelves of books, and a vastly different social orientation (although it would be decades before I had the vocabulary to express it). Fascinating, but very different. Grandma Lamb was a bubbly, easy to like woman. Grandpa Lamb was somewhat introverted, intellectual, and unknowable. My visits to their house were pleasant but also strangely uncomfortable. I was always happy to get back to the Negri house where things were, if not always harmonious, at least what I was accustomed to.

So here we were at the rinkydink airport in our rinkydink town, all together, to welcome the man who was an actor, stepping off the plane from New York City. Here was the man whom, at an earlier age, I had longed to see again. Now at the age of ten, I would have preferred that he didn't exist. It was just that uncomfortable.

After an initial awkward embrace, Dad reached into a bag and pulled out a box containing a model airplane kit. It was big; bigger than any toy plane I'd ever seen. He said, "I picked this up on the way. I thought it looked interesting." I didn't say anything.

In the years since this encounter, I have often reflected on my amazing inexperience at that time. I honestly had no idea whether or not it was a gift for me. I looked at the depiction on the box. Dad said, "Maybe we can put it together tomorrow." My brain slipped into high gear. *He said he got it because it looked interesting. It must be his. He must be trying to share **his** project of building this thing.*

I didn't take the box in my hands. There was another awkward period of silence, awkward for both of us. The box was suspended in air as he held it for a few moments, then put it back in the bag.

Thinking back now on this, I can only compare this exchange with that which would have taken place with Grandpa Negri: "Hey, Cristofero, here's-a something for you. You like? Ha! ha! Hey, d'joo eat yet?" Spirited, vibrant, and definitely familiar. Nothing like the detached, intellectual, colorless expression of that other side of my family.

I dreaded the next few days.

When we saw each other again the next day, Dad sat on the floor of his parents' porch and helped me take all the parts of the model plane out of the box. The body snapped together and didn't require glue, which was fortunate, since I had been unsuccessful at putting even one model together in my short life. He had to fit the wings on the body; I couldn't do it. The propeller was powered by a rubber band that stretched the entire length of the inside of the plane. Dad had me wind it up and we took it into the front yard. With a shove, he let it go and it became airborne…for a time. It made a rapid and sudden nosedive into the grass. Repeated tries had the same result. It would not fly any distance. The "interesting" device was set aside and we went inside to eat.

The dinner was only slightly less uncomfortable. The first aspect that was different from what I was used to was that the Lamb family actually ate in a dining room. We ate at the kitchen table. There was a decorative centerpiece on the tablecloth; I had no idea the concept even existed. The Lambs had a number of various size dishes to contain the numerous items that made up the meal; we typically ate everything off one plate, sometimes with a second smaller plate or bowl for a side dish, if there was one.

At the Negri house, we usually had a big pot of something and you got yourself enough helpings—from the stovetop—to satisfy you. There was no thought of a "balanced diet" any more than there was room for a vase of flowers in the center of the table. Here, there was Beef Stroganoff, salad, some kind of potatoes, green beans, sliced bread, and the various serving bowls were passed around from person to person. This made me uneasy. I had no schooling in table etiquette and had no experience with this communal ritual. I was scared I would spill things, and my mother wisely took over for me after the bread came around.

The food was weird, too. Unfamiliar shapes and textures, bland flavor. I picked at it a bit and couldn't wait to go home.

As Mom and I got ready to leave, Dad gave me a couple small photographs of him, cut from a contact sheet. They were test shots for a television commercial he did. They were fascinating. There he was, my Dad, holding a cigarette and looking past the camera at something in the distance. The lighting, the non-existent background, the pose—this was the kind of photo you saw in the magazines, or stills from movies. It had not the slightest resemblance to the kind of picture one took of a friend who was smiling at the camera, with the light evenly dispersed (or worse yet, ricocheting off his glasses), and a tree limb or other object seemingly growing out of his head. Professional photography. I was impressed. My father is one of those guys on TV!

In actuality, he would work on the stage far more than he would in television, and like most actors he would work far less than he would like. But he was achieving the dreams that he pursued after splitting up with Mom. He would write me every so often. His letters were like letters one would write to an adult. After I got older, I wondered if it was because he wanted to treat me like an adult, or if he just had no idea how to relate to a kid.

There would be a couple more visits from Dad in my childhood. They were essentially the same; uncomfortable affairs that made me want to retreat to the City Market, with its seedy but colorful people, simple food consumed in booths of varnished wood with no tablecloth or flowers or anyone saying grace before digging in.

Not having a father around didn't have much impact on my development, but I was acutely embarrassed at having it known. If an adult innocently asked about my father, I would just clam up. Things like a father-and-son picnic, or Father's Day, made me feel panicky.

Around this time I started getting allergy shots once a week at a doctor's office in our neighborhood. He was a gerontologist, and had no child patients, but Grandpa asked him to be my doctor since my old doctor had moved away. Dr. Curry liked Grandpa and agreed. So once a week, I would sit in the reception room with a bunch of elderly people, waiting to get my injection. They seemed to enjoy having a ten year-old in their midst. One little man used to smile at me and try to make me laugh. He had a cute, puckish smile. I liked him. He once asked me to help him track down where the hidden speaker for the piped-in music was. A cute little man.

Then one day he unexpectedly asked me, "Who's your father?" I looked down at the floor. He asked again. I didn't say anything. It seemed as if anything I could say would lead to an endless stream of uncomfortable questions

—"Where does he live?" "Are your parents divorced?" "Why did they split up?" I kept silent.

"Who's your father?" The question came yet again. He was being persistent. I slid off the black wooden Hitchcock chair and left the reception room.

I didn't like the cute little man anymore.

8

We were in Ohio! Not a boast worthy of even an adolescent like me, but it was exciting because for the first time I got to see the famous Saint Rocco picnic. Mom, Grandpa, and I drove to Warren, Ohio for the annual event that Grandpa had been attending by himself for many years. The weekend closest to August 16th was when the reunion of the *Societa di Collolonghese* was held. Those who came to America from the little mountain town of Collelongo would converge with their families upon this northeastern Ohio city in August, near to the Feast Day of Saint Rocco, the patron saint of the town. They had been doing this for decades.

Grandpa had driven himself for years, sometimes taking a friend along, sometimes riding with a friend. In the last year, he had had a couple events that undermined his confidence in driving. He sideswiped a parked car and a few weeks after, backed into another car while parking. I remember overhearing the conversation after that when Mom told Connie "Daddy's not going to drive anymore." He didn't drive all that often anyway. It didn't seem to me to be a major change in the world. But the end result was that now I was at the reunion!

I didn't have the insight then to wonder how different it might be for Grandpa to have us along. I looked at photos from earlier picnic weekends and saw some signs of merriment, but mostly a lot of obviously Italian people standing around talking with their hands. When we got to Warren, we went to a bar/restaurant called Café 422. There I saw more overt signs of merriment.

The owner of the 422 was one of the organizers of the yearly event, and secretary of the Collelongo Society. He was warm and welcoming, genuinely glad to see Grandpa again and gracious to Mom and me. The place was filled with revelers having drinks in a pre-picnic party the night before. Dozens of Italian men—boisterous, laughing, conversing in the mother tongue—were buying each other drinks and intermittently confirming to each other: *"Domani*, eh?" *"Domani*!" was the hearty reply, with a lift of the glass. It was clear that these people couldn't wait for tomorrow's events.

Joining us for dinner was Grandpa's best friend, who lived there in Warren. Augusto di Scenna, known to us by his nickname "Gianghetto", was a tiny man who had also come from Collelongo. He sat next to me in our circular booth, and his eyes were almost level with my twelve year-old eyes. He appeared youthful because of his small size, but tonight he was bemoaning his descent into old age. *"Una Beera,"* he said, regarding the beer bottle in his hand, *"… inebriato!"* Drunk on one beer. Grandpa smiled broadly, showing off the new dentures he had acquired only a month before. He looked good.

I was allowed anything on the menu and I spotted frog legs and thought that was an appropriate meal for a departure from the ordinary. You can get a cheeseburger anywhere. And there will certainly be enough pasta to be had tomorrow. Yes, I want to try frog legs, I said.

While we were waiting for our food, there was a short discussion of frog legs and their tendency to jump around after being divided from the frog. I started regretting my decision and the wait became increasingly worrying. Grandpa and Gianghetto (pronounced like "John get") caught each other up on their lives and who had died in the last year, etc. Mom watched the merry-makers who spilled into the dining room from the bar, laughing and embracing each other. I just sat and watched a more and more clear picture form in my head, of horrible disembodied legs twitching and jumping off my plate. They couldn't still move, could they?

When everybody's dinners arrived, mine appeared to be just a benign pile of skinny breaded-and-fried drumsticks. I didn't detect any movement. All the same, I watched them for quite a while. Grandpa said, "Aren't you gonna eat your frog legs?" I made an unconvincing reply. "Um…I'm waiting for them to cool down." Gianghetto looked at me out of the corner of his eye, smiled a wry smile, and went back to stabbing at his food with verve.

I liked the look of the Café 422. I was especially fascinated with the barroom side, part of which was visible from where we were seated. The lighting, the wood grain of the bar itself, the impeccably attired bartenders with their white shirts and bow ties, the glass block window…it was everything the City Market was not. All the same elements were there: the counter, the stools, the people drinking and talking. But our bar was fiberboard. Theirs was mahogany. Our back bar had stained glass panels, mostly covered up by calendars, beer ads, and aspirin placards. Theirs had fluted glass panels with colored lights behind them. Beautiful.

And the people. It may be just a matter of how many drinks separate the civilized drinker from the common drunkard, but there was definitely a different crowd bending the elbow here. It was certainly not a "Long Branch Saloon," as my mother often called our store; a reference to the *Gunsmoke* TV show.

That always cracked me up. She was right. The seedy characters in the Long Branch Saloon in each week's show had direct kinship with the City Market customers. I never saw anyone with impeccable dress or refined manners ever enter the City Market, and maybe they didn't enter the Café 422 that often, but nonetheless this was a different world and I spent a lot of time taking it all in.

I finally got up the courage to eat the frog legs and arrived at the same conclusion that adults do when they try some unidentifiable protein. "It tastes like chicken," I said.

Later, I had the first experience of staying in a hotel room by myself. It was the perfect compliment to being out at a nice place like the 422. I pretended that I had been on the other side, the barroom, all evening and now I had retired to my personal room in the hotel. The bathroom had a shower. The only place I had experienced one was at the municipal swimming pool. This was much nicer. I got in and took a shower that lasted half an hour.

The next day, the celebrations began at a park that had been reserved exclusively for the reunion. Dozens of families had tables where they would lay out all kinds of foods, and everyone would share with anyone who came by their table. It was amazing how many variations there were on the same familiar dishes. I got to taste a lot of different spaghetti sauces and it reminded me once more of how completely different the pasta tasted if we ate at Aunt Jennie's house. How different could Grandma and her sister make the same thing? *Well, it's like that everywhere*, I supposed.

Bottles of wine were on most family tables, and a bar was set up for those who wanted beer or liquor. The makeshift style of this was a real contrast to the bar of the 422 the night before.

There were men everywhere challenging each other to play *mora*, the Italian equivalent of rock-paper-scissors that I'd seen occasionally. I got to participate in my first game of *bocce*. This was one game involving a ball that I didn't mind.

Gianghetto scampered around from place to place in his youthful way. I met my third cousin Enrico for the first time (I tried to follow the logic of Grandpa's first cousin being my *third* cousin). There was Mister DiLoretto, who had such a distinctive face that he became for me a landmark figure at the picnic in the years to come. His heavy eyebrows, deep smile lines, and dark skin made him look to me a little like an Indian chief without his bonnet. His hair parted in the middle, and thick strands would gradually make their way down to dangle at both temples as he consumed glass after glass of wine and he looked gradually more and more unkempt.

Grandpa mixed with old friends and visited tables, eventually just planting himself in one spot and carrying on conversations with people who came and went. Their language was fast and animated, and I didn't understand a word of it. I was disappointed. Why, only last night I had understood "*inebriato*"! Somehow I expected to be able to extract more from the mother tongue being spoken so freely there, but I was mistaken.

Grandpa was a curious mix of gentility and down-to-earth peasant manners. He held his cup with his pinky extended, in a most courtly fashion. Then, when his cup was empty, he slurped up the coffee that had spilled over into the saucer.

Mom saw him raise the saucer to his lips and said "Oh!" in a disgusted whisper to herself, perhaps worrying that I was going to follow his example. All it did for me was provide another round of adolescent chuckles.

In the evening, a band played. People danced. At the end there were fireworks. At the grand finale, as the sky filled with colorful explosions, people shouted "Viva San Rocco!"

The next morning, Mom piloted the car back toward familiar old Morgantown. I spent most of my time in the back seat thinking of the Café 422.

Fun in Warren, Ohio. Al Flenniken (center) drove Grandpa this year.

Grandpa at the picnic.

9

Townies. That's what I called them. Not an original name, but when you used it, everyone knew what you meant. They were the peculiar characters who haunted the downtown area, the ones you would see on any given day who had some quality that set them apart from the mainstream. Probably because of the collection of interesting personalities I became familiar with at the City Market, I was sensitized to this element of society. I noticed these people with their oddities before my friends did; I made up nicknames for them and actually popularized some of them in my circle.

For some reason, I didn't consider the customers at the City Market to be townies. Although many of them qualified by virtue of their idiosyncrasies, they didn't hang around on the main street and, I guess, felt more like family than the odd assortment of vagrants and oddballs I had to pass in order to get to the store.

Even Ronnie Kline from across the street was technically a townie in my book. His family's furniture store was between the Sportsman's Bar and the "Salivation" Army. Ronnie was mildly retarded and walked up and down the sidewalk pleasantly talking to people. He was childlike, with a soft, slow way of speaking. He would ask a stranger his name, and then when the reply came, he took out a pen and wrote the name on a handkerchief. That handkerchief had dozens of names scrawled on it. Ronnie did not qualify as a townie because he was afflicted, but because he was just around town a lot.

Other townies were in a different category.

There was, for example, Puppet Man. He had some neurological problem, I guess, that made his movements look as though he was being controlled by someone else. He was eclipsed, though, by Marionette Man, whose erratic motions were much more dramatic, and really looked as if someone was pulling invisible strings on his limbs from above. His foot would rise at least twelve inches off the ground before he took a step. He always wore painter's clothes, and I imagine the damage came from the paint back then, which was pretty toxic.

There was Glove Man, who wore a pair of thick gloves on his hands but only an undershirt—all year around. He didn't do anything else odd, but he really didn't need to. I would see him walking downtown often.

Then there were the newspaper vendors, who had their own corners and their own individual styles. There was Duck (I don't think I was the first to christen him thus), who had webbed hands and feet, and walked in a kind of splayed waddle. His face was flat and his bug eyes were widely spaced. He always wore a cloth cap just like the newsies of a generation before. He had the kind of appearance that made you want to look elsewhere so he wouldn't think you were staring. Someone told me once that he was that way because his mother had syphilis. He called out, "Paaaay-perrr," and this was a frequent sound downtown.

A guy named Jimmy, who sold papers in the 200 block of High Street, was equally afflicted. He had had polio (as the story goes, but it seems likely), and walked in very short shuffling steps. One arm was drawn, and his balding head was egg-shaped and leaned slightly to one side. Jimmy had a great newsboy's call: "Pay-YAY-per!   Get your

Morgantown POST!" He would repeat this over and over, and you could hear him for blocks. I think he was the most successful of the downtown vendors.

There was also Wesley, who had no endearing qualities whatsoever. Grizzled, dirty, gruff, he would shove a folded newspaper in your face as you passed, hoarsely saying "Paper?" He spat on the sidewalk constantly, and there was usually dribble at the corner of his mouth. He was gross. He stood at the corner of High and Walnut Streets and I often crossed to the other side just to avoid him. But he belonged in the townie directory no matter how I felt about him.

Then there was a benevolent soul in the form of Mr. Riley. The opposite corner of that same intersection where Wesley was busy spitting on the sidewalk was the most dangerous corner in town. There was really no way to safely negotiate that part of Walnut Street in those days before crossing signs were installed. Traffic turning down Walnut from High Street was constant, and if you wanted to cross there, you had to get lucky because if you waited for one street to get a red light, the traffic from the other came barreling down at you. There was no letup. Adults had a hard time, and when school let out in the afternoons, kids had to dart out whenever they could, their short legs working overtime to pass this hurdle.

But longtime resident Don Riley took it upon himself to remedy this. He posted himself there at mid-afternoon, and would stop traffic for the kids to cross. The Police Department never posted an officer there, to my recollection, and it was sorely needed. Mr. Riley's service caused a controversy that got some newspaper attention. The Police did not appreciate Riley's showing them up and ordered him to desist. When he didn't, they arrested him one day. This set off a small community uproar. Mr. Riley reappeared at the corner, assisting people once more at the dangerous intersection in his long raincoat, old hat and worn-out shoes. To some, he was an old drunk with delusions of grandeur. To others, he was a sad but comical sight.

Still others, like myself, saw him as something of a hero. As an adolescent I hoped my future adult self would have the courage to do the right thing despite what people would say about me. I certainly didn't have that kind of guts then. The kind of strength and nobility embodied by the comic book characters I idolized seemed at once attainable and yet impossible. At that age, social acceptance was so important; yet, I did none of the things that won other kids acclaim. I didn't play any sports, wasn't popular in school…so I retreated, like lots of other kids, into the world of comic books. And in that regard, Pleasant Street was kind to me once more, for it offered Walters' Newsstand.

Walters' Newsstand had once been on the opposite corner of the old City Market, I was told. Their building was torn down, too; they moved up a block while we moved down. The place was a magic haven, much like the movie theaters where we kids would go to the Saturday matinees. A trip to the movies would leave you with ideas and images in your head after you went home. But a trip to Walters' Newsstand left you with tangible images that would not fade with time, and ideas that could be renewed an infinite number of times, simply by turning the page. I went there every Saturday, and I mean *every* Saturday. It was such an important part of my week that I would deliberately pace myself so that I didn't buy all my month's reading material at once. I wanted something waiting there for me next Saturday. By the time I had exhausted all my favorites, the next month's issues would be out.

I started, as most kids do, with the "funny animal" books, progressing to the super-hero comics as I got older, then adding monster magazines in my adolescence, which coincided with a monster craze in the U.S. in the mid-1960s. Then surreptitious examinations of Playboy became part of a trip to Walters'. Each type of periodical necessitated moving from rack to rack, farther to the right as you progressed, which was lucky because it put you out of sight of the owners by the time you got to Playboy status. The racks of paperback books stood between the front counter and the lurid stuff, and I would squat down, pretending to look at the magazines on the bottom shelf.

Jack Walters didn't mind if you stood there and read all day, and I'm sure now he knew when someone like me was looking at the "adult" magazines. I was smart about it; I would come up front after a while and buy a bottle of soda pop. Then back to the magazines. When I brought the empty bottle back, I would get a bag of peanuts. That way, I thought, it would always seem like I was just starting to browse. Ha!

Jack was a great guy. Everybody liked him. He laughed and talked with the customers, some of whom popped in only long enough to buy a paper, and others who would linger and chat. There were regulars at the newsstand, just like at the City Market, and I was proud to be one of them. But one of them was a bona-fide townie that everybody knew: Crazy John Moore.

On this particular Saturday, I was headed for the newsstand when I encountered John Moore walking the opposite way.

I knew what was coming, because I had been through it before. "Get over there!" he yelled. He gestured frantically with his hands. "Get over on your own side of the sidewalk!" I was not the only one who was lectured on sidewalk etiquette; he did this with many people. He would cross a street at the light and yell at the stopped cars as though they were not fully stopped. He would express outrage that drivers pointed their cars in his direction. He was the anti-Riley. Instead of helping people cross, he chased them away.

Now I was happily browsing magazines at Walters'. John Moore came in. He bought a bottle of chocolate milk and was going on about the Pirates. He was a big Pittsburgh Pirates fan, and typically had a transistor radio pressed to his ear as he walked around. Jack chatted with him politely. It's hard to describe Crazy John's speech pattern. He stammered a little; he was blustery and sounded angry even when he wasn't scolding anyone. I stayed behind the paperback bookracks, not wanting another confrontation with him (no super-hero courage yet, alas). When he had gone, a customer said to Jack, "Why, that guy's nuts!" Obviously, he wasn't a downtown regular. Jack's laughing reply, in his distinctive raspy voice, was "Why do you think they call him *Crazy* John?"

I bought the latest issue of *Castle of Frankenstein* Magazine, said goodbye to Jack, and walked down Pleasant Street to the store for some lunch. Grandpa greeted me when I came in and told me to fix myself some hot dogs. I had gained a modicum of regard by this time, to the extent that they let me make hot dogs sometimes for the customers. Grandma even gave me the task of chopping the onions for the hot dog table when I was around. But I never reached competence in drawing a beer. Anytime a customer asked me for a refill and I tried to do it, it would just come out all foam. Grandma would just make a dissatisfied sound and grab the glass away from me. She would never tell me how to do it right. The mysteries of the beer tap would bedevil me for years to come.

But today I was above such concerns. I made myself a couple hot dogs with chili and onions, took them to the last booth, and opened *Castle of Frankenstein*. I was having a ball. I was halfway through my second hot dog when I looked up to see Snyder. He was a regular at the City Market, known only by his last name, and a talkative fellow. He said, "Eatin' hot dogs, are you?" I smiled. I never had enough folksiness in me to make that kind of small talk. Then he said something that interested me. "Next time, put some hot sauce on 'em. They're real good that way."

A bottle of Frank's Hot Sauce stood beside all the other condiments on the stainless steel hot dog table as well as on top of the bar, but for some reason I never before that moment considered sampling it. I got up and made myself two more hot dogs, this time with hot sauce, and yes! They were indeed good that way.

Sitting in the next booth were two of the small number of women who ever drank beer in the store. They were laughing about something. I never knew their names. One was tallish and husky, usually wearing a scarf over her head. Her friend was a very skinny woman who had a drooping mouth, chain-smoked cigarettes, and always seemed to have a sore on her face somewhere. She was very unhealthy-looking, and watching that mouth with a glass up to it made me want to add more bleach to the sterilizing basin in the bar sink. She sort of turned my stomach.

But I was watching today because two men had entered the store and walked back to their booth. Mom had talked about how the woman with the scarf went around with both her husband and her boyfriend, and I wanted a closer look at this interesting arrangement. The two men sat opposite the women and ordered beers. One was older, but neither was young by any means. I decided the older one was the husband.

The City Market, pioneer gathering place for alternative lifestyles!

In one booth farther up was a solitary individual. I hadn't noticed him when I came in. Now I saw who it was, and was surprised. It was Shadow. Grandma had named him that. I hadn't seen him in years. He had been a regular when I was very young. I had forgotten about him. He was older now, much heavier, but still recognizable. And he still gave me the creeps.

"He suffered shell shock in the war," I was told. He looked something like Bela Lugosi, in one of those old movies when Bela was turning on the spook factor and his eyes would bore a hole in you. Shadow's eyes had a similar quality, but unlike Lugosi's, they were sunken in the middle of dark circles. His dominant expression was intense, and his mouth hung open a lot. I remembered his sitting there in that booth years before, chuckling to himself until the laughter rose and consumed him; he would be laughing hysterically, loudly, insanely—and then the fit would end. It was scary.

Now, although he still looked disturbed, he had a softer look all around. Apparently he had been "away" for some time and now was considered stable enough to be back in society.

He sat quietly and drank his beer, then got up to leave. Grandma smiled and pleasantly said goodbye. I watched him walk out the door. When I turned around, everyone else was watching him, too.

I went back to *Castle of Frankenstein* Magazine, looked at some pictures, and pondered the differences and similarities between the spooky guys I loved to watch in the movies and the spooky guys I encountered downtown and in the store. I thought of Voo Tavoo. If I had a movie camera, I thought, I could make a heck of a thriller.

I got ready to go after a while. Grandpa reached up to change the channel on the TV set. I said I'd see him at home later. "Huh?" he said, as usual. I repeated, and left.

Walking up Spruce Street toward home, I remembered that Mom said if I wanted a ride I should come to the beauty shop where she was getting her hair done. There I was, right in front of the Beauty College when I remembered, so I went in. Most boys my age wouldn't have been caught dead going in there, but there was one beautician training there who had cut my mother's hair a few times I thought was really cute. Tina. She had black hair cut in a pageboy style and blue eyes and, well, I was at that age where I started noticing these things. When I went in, the place smelled like burnt hair and chemicals and perfume. The owner, Mrs. Morgan, was ringing up a customer and I took a seat in the lobby where I could see into the front room where the hair dryers were.

There was Mom, with her head under the contraption that looked like the nose of a rocket, a magazine in her hand like all the other women in the row of chairs there. She saw me, then looked back at her magazine. Connie was nowhere in sight. I paced around a little, looked through the doorway into the large room in the back where the beauty stations were, and saw Tina. She was talking to one of the other beauticians. She smiled and waved. What a doll. She came walking over.

"Waiting for your mom?" she asked. "She'll be a little while longer."

"Yeah, just hanging around, like…" My voice trailed off because I didn't know what else to say. I wanted to deflect the image of me as someone's kid; of course I couldn't dispel it, but I wanted to be recognized as my own person, someone Tina herself would be interested in (even despite the difference in our years, which didn't seem like a barrier then—was I delusional!).

I walked outside and waited for a while on the porch of the house-turned-beauty school. Unlike most residential homes in the area, the porch was brick with a clay tile floor. It had been a fraternity house when I was younger. I never knew what the Greek letters stood for, but I always noticed the skull and crossbones mounted next to the front door. Cool. A couple years before, the beauty college bought the place and Mom and Connie had been getting their hair done here on Saturdays since.

After I had been out on the porch for a minute, Tina came out. "Where ya goin'?" I asked. "Just to the house. Wanna come?"

"Sure," I said, trying not to sound too anxious. One part of me was jumping up and down in triumph at my luck, and another part was hoping to get away to avoid the awkwardness. I walked with her around to the rear of the building, to a house where some of the Beauty School girls lived. We went in the rear door and two of the girls were sitting at a table in the kitchen. They were singing along to a song on the radio. Tina opened the refrigerator, got a couple things out, and offered me a Pepsi. "No thanks," I said, "I'm not in the Pepsi generation" (The advertising slogan at that time was "Come Alive! You're in the Pepsi generation"). Tina laughed. I thought to myself, "That wasn't half bad for coolness." I stayed a minute, then I walked back to the front, where Mom and Connie were waiting. Mom was annoyed that she had to wait for me. How long could she have been waiting? The three of us walked across the street to the parking lot and entered the car for the ride home.

From the back seat, I stared at Mom's head. Her hair was teased up into the usual grotesque, inflated shape. Once we got home, she did what she did every time: spent ten minutes in the bathroom combing it all out. Once she emerged, it always looked like it did before she went to the salon. I didn't get it.

Connie did her usual thing. She waited until she had an audience and then made a big show of picking up several pieces of lint from the throw rug in the hall. Sighing loudly, she picked up one, then two tiny pieces of fuzz from the rug, dramatically put them in her other palm, and bent forward to retrieve more debris. "Nobody cleans in this house," she said to nobody and everybody. My mother's face got that sharp look and she put her hands on her hips. *Here it comes*, I thought.

"Oh, you think *you* keep this house clean?"

Connie straightened up and glared at her. "Tsk!" Connie made the *tsk* sound louder and more often than anyone. I quickly exited. As I left, the voices were rising in the usual progression as Mom reminded Connie of the hours that she worked and the hours that Grandma and Grandpa put in at the store, and what did Connie do? As I stepped off the front porch, I heard her say that Connie never even changed the roll of toilet paper when it was empty, which made me laugh. Because it was true.

I hated the arguing and I had reason to hate it often, because it happened often. As I walked down the street, the thought suddenly occurred to me: There was some kind of link between Crazy John and Connie. Was there really any difference between someone who makes a big display of straightening a rug and picking up lint in order to disparage others, and someone who berates you for taking up space on the sidewalk that he thinks he is entitled to? There wasn't much difference to my mind. That drive to complain and be argumentative, to invent controversy when none existed, was pure craziness in my book. After all, didn't they call him "Crazy" John? But I never before had the idea that if Connie applied her antics downtown, she would have been a townie. The realization made me giggle.

I entered the corner Laundromat to wait out the screaming match. I thought about Tina. What a sweetheart.

10

As I passed through my teenage years, I was given a task here and there that I was deemed capable of performing (unlike pouring a beer, in which I had proven myself incompetent). If I were at the store when the weekly order from the wholesaler came in, I would unpack the boxes and stock the shelves. The item I remember most clearly was the tinned sardines. This was before the pull-top that is common for canned foods now; there was a metal "key" lightly soldered to the bottom of the can that the buyer would snap off and use to peel back the metal cover. I stacked the flat cans for display on a case in the front of the store, in two piles. Blue label: packed in water. Pink label: packed in oil. We sold a lot of sardines. To this day, they are a favorite of mine.

Tony Colasante came in the store. He was an old man from "the old country", and he walked slowly, with a cane. He smiled at me as I looked out from behind a pile of boxes. He wore a long, wrinkly, dirty raincoat and smoked skinny little Italian cigars that looked something like the "Slim Jim" smoked sausages that we sold from the bar top. In fact, once I was inspired to park a piece of Slim Jim in the corner of my mouth to simulate a cigar, until Grandma said something about it and I quickly chewed it up.

I finished stacking the sardines, put the shipment of cereal and toilet paper on the shelves, and I was ready for one other task I was trusted to perform. "Call Tony a cab," Grandma said to me. Tony handed me a dime and said, as he always did, "It's-a two nine-a two, three three three six." I knew the number of the taxicab office from previous times calling it for him. I knew what to tell the dispatcher, where he was going. "Ten minutes" was the reply. I told Tony. He thanked me. I'm not sure why he was not capable of calling himself. He walked slowly to the front of the store to wait. A skinny little Italian man with a skinny little Italian cigar.

At the bar, Hugh Runner was talking to the man next to him about something, in his oratorical voice. I noticed Doctor Miller at the end of the bar, having a bottle of beer and looking at the TV set. He would stop in at the City Market on his walk home from the office at the end of the workday. Two things were predictable about Doctor Miller. He never drank draft beer, preferring a bottle. And he never sat on a stool. He usually stood at the far end of the bar. "He's an osteopath," Grandma said once, "and he doesn't think he should sit down." I made a quizzical face and she clarified: "He's a back doctor." I never knew if he had a back problem or if he was just philosophically opposed to sitting, but it was another example of how every person at the City Market was different. He spoke to me, upended his bottle, and started for the door, having had his single daily beer.

Hugh Runner called me over. He had something for me, he said. He reached into a leather case he carried, and produced a thick sheaf of bound papers that looked like a newspaper of some kind, but it was stapled on the side. I looked closer. It said "Congressional Record" at the top, in Old English script. Hugh was talking all the while I examined it. It was, he said, a very instructive thing for a young man. He had brought it down to the store for me because it was educational. I thumbed through it as he talked, and it was almost like looking at a newspaper printed in an unfamiliar language. Oh, I understood the words all right, but everywhere I looked were phrases like "Final deliberations in closed session, subsequent to approval of those statements..." and "Deemed in compliance which would permit a Senator to release information to the public, *blah blah, blah.*" Nowhere did I come across anything that said anything concrete. I managed a half smile, and he told me of all the all the advantages of being more informed about legislation than the other boys my age. I thanked him for the gift, hoping that would end the conversation, but it didn't. Grandma didn't come to my rescue like she would if someone like Mac was bothering Hugh!

And—think of the devil—Mac himself walked in at this juncture. He got a bottle of beer and took his place in a booth and I hoped he would come over and take my place with Hugh, who had got up a good head of steam and was now in high gear. "Of course," he said, "the House and Senate journals contain only the votes and results, *not* the debates and discussions, which are contained here and are of great interest, although they may be revised and do not always appear verbatim, *blah blah blah…*" Geez.

I thanked him again for the swell pile of words and put it on the table in the back room, on top of my copy of *Castle of Frankenstein* Magazine.

I watched through the peephole for a while to see who was coming in and going out. Hugh Runner remained at the far end of the bar. Maybe I wouldn't go back out until he was gone. A man I didn't know was standing in Doctor Miller's spot at the end closest to the partition I was looking through. He was looking up at the TV and eating a pickled egg. I couldn't see Mac in his booth because of the egg eater. Mmmm…pickled eggs.

In the next booth I could see Snyder and his family. This guy would actually bring his wife and kids to the City Market. Snyder got up and came to the bar for service. I decided to go out and tell him that I tried his suggestion about hot sauce on chili dogs.

Snyder said hello and asked me to get him another beer. Grandma was busy with someone in the front of the store. My chance! I grabbed the glass, positioned it under the tap, and pulled the lever back with a smooth motion. I angled the glass better than usual, but there was still quite a bit of foam. I looked over and Grandma was scowling from the front counter. I poured some of the foam off and added some more beer, but it looked just the same as before. "Oh, that's all right," said Snyder. Just then, the man who ate the pickled egg knocked his empty beer bottle over with his elbow, scrambled to right it, and knocked it over again there on the bar top. He swayed a little as he stood there for a second, then walked unsteadily to the exit. Snyder watched him with an amused look on his face.

"Oh, he's not feelin' no pain, is he?" Snyder said. "Heh heh". His eyes twinkled. I smiled.

"Oh, when I was in the army I was stationed in France, you know, during the war," he said, "and we had ourselves a lot of wine to drink. Oh, we couldn't see straight! The next mornin' we woke up feelin' just awful." He leaned over the bar as though the story was about to get more private. "We was all thirsty, but I knew not to drink any water before I had somethin' to eat. I went across the street and got me some breakfast, but those guys, they didn't listen to me and they drank water."

I was curious now.

"Well, that water just made 'em drunk again! I was OK, because I ate something."

"The water made them drunk?" I asked. The reply came: "Yep. The water turns into alcohol. But I knew better. They was in trouble but not me!"

I thought to myself, *this might be valuable knowledge.* "So," Snyder said, "if you ever have too much to drink, don't drink no water. Get yourself something to eat and you'll be fine."

Grandma appeared from out of nowhere and said to Snyder, "All right, leave him alone." Snyder went back to his booth and I thought, *Hey, at least this man's telling me something interesting. Where were you when I was trapped by that Congress guy?*

I wonder how my life would have been different if Hugh Runner had made the Congressional Record seem more interesting than Snyder's World War II stories. I might have spent my twenties getting a law degree, instead of unsuccessfully trying to fend off hangovers by not drinking water!

At least I learned a valuable lesson in the dangers of hearsay evidence.

Mac and Hugh have a discourse.

11

A sunny Friday afternoon in the after-school hours. Autumn was here. Temperature getting cooler. I got off the high school bus downtown, feeling elated. No school for a few days! I saw Duck going down the street in the distance, his splay-footed gait recognizable. "Paaaaay-per!" I said to myself, chuckling.

As I walked down the main street on my way to the store, I passed by another grocery store, a landmark business right in the middle of downtown. Like our store, there were bushel baskets of items propped up on wooden boxes on the sidewalk out front. Beans, onions, chestnuts, and onion sets were there, with metal scoops in the tilted baskets and paper bags to scoop them into. The honor system was in force— you would get what you wanted and take it into the store to be weighed. In that regard it was just like our place.

The front windows had signs advertising the daily or weekly specials. These signs, with professionally painted lettering on butcher paper, were common in markets then. Typically, they used blue and red ink, and were painted with brushes by steady hands. The signs were taped to the windows and the large letters were legible from some distance. The only trouble was that I spotted two errors in spelling. I realized that I often saw spelling mistakes in their signs. "Bread" would be "bred". "Spinach" would be "spinuch". Even though the signs changed every week or two, some new sign would have a new error. I knew the signs were painted by commercial artists and not the grocer himself, so I was curious as to why this would be.

I thought about it all the way to the City Market. I entered the store, set down my schoolbooks, and mentioned the spelling matter to Grandma. She said, "Oh, he's been doing that for years."

"What, making mistakes in spelling?" I asked. Grandma smiled. "Those aren't mistakes. He has it done deliberately."

I smiled skeptically and said, "He wants mistakes in his signs? What kind of business is that?"

She dunked another glass in the sink basin and said, looking down at the sink, "Somebody like you passes by and reads the sign. He sees the mistake and goes into the store to tell them that the sign is wrong. When he's in there, Mike says 'try this new cheese—we just got it in' and hands him a slice. The man tastes it while he's taking Mike out to show him the mistake. Mike thanks him and says 'Wasn't that good? Want to take some home?' And now he's made a sale that he wouldn't have before."

Grandma went on washing glasses. The smile was gone from her face. I was dumbfounded. I couldn't believe that such a far-fetched scheme would actually work, and yet I knew, having been in the store and seeing the owner, that it probably did work. That store was a prosperous one. It was not just its better location that achieved it, because in the same block was the Sanitary Market, owned by one of Grandpa's countrymen, and that store didn't sell any more groceries than did our store. They had a minimal amount of inventory and did not have the beer trade to support them like we did. Mike's store didn't serve beer, either; but he had something that the others did not have—cunning. The devious tricks that added just a few more dollars had paid off over time.

I was to see this contrast between the stores displayed in a telling exchange that evening at home. I heard Grandpa ask Grandma, "Anything today?" She replied, not looking at him, "Don't ask."

"Huh?" was the predictable response. "Don't ask!" she repeated in a louder, fatalistic tone. There was no more conversation between them that night. I wasn't sure at first, but contemplating the matter I decided "Anything today?" must mean "Did we make any money today?" and it was my first inkling that the store was not a profitable venture. As a kid, there was no reason to think about it. Now I was growing up, and the harsh realities of life would no longer be hidden from me.

I felt strangely morose about the whole thing. I walked out onto the front porch, stood there for a while, then walked down the street to Ralph's house. He was sitting on his front steps. I sat down beside him and we made a few conversational sounds but no real conversation. Maybe he felt the same as I did that night. The air got cooler, too cool to stay there on the concrete steps comfortably, so we said goodnight.

The next day was Saturday. Not just an ordinary Saturday, but a home game day. The University football games had the effect of transforming the town into a beehive of frenetic motion. Today's game was with one of the school's longtime rival teams, but it didn't mean anything to me. I had no interest in sports, and especially not football, which seemed to me to be the crudest of the crude. My view of football fans was the same as everyone else's picture of people who went to prize fights, or frequented pool halls—rough, cigar-smoking, whiskey-breathed loudmouths who screamed "Kill 'em!" and flew into a rage over any official's call against their home team, even if deserved. Our team won? They're the greatest. They lost? We were robbed. The attitude made me crazy. There seemed to be nothing *sporting* about the sport.

But the existence—the *presence*—of the football games was another thing entirely. It was a dynamic background to Saturdays in the fall; with the stadium just a mile from our house and the voice of the announcer and the roar of the crowd carried on the wind and plainly heard from our street. Hundreds of people converged on our town who normally weren't here; alumni and sports fans packed the hotels and populated the sidewalks, and sometimes they included friends of the family, like today. Several out-of-town friends had come to see the game and would visit our home afterward.

I, too, was going to the game. Not to *see* the game, mind you, but to experience the game day atmosphere. Mom was assistant to the Athletic Director, and was able to provide me with a ticket if I wanted one. This day I wanted one. My school friends who loved football were annoyed that I, the sports hater, could attend whenever I wanted. My mother was annoyed that I had such disdain for the Athletic Department "that has fed and clothed you all these years." But no amount of animosity from any direction was going to dampen my spirits. It was Saturday!

The real appeal of game days was the opportunity to observe and fantasize about a certain lifestyle—the collegiate lifestyle—and it was most evident at those home games where fraternity brothers sat together and cheered and young lovers sat close and held hands. In those days before blue jeans were *de rigueur*, football game dates were marked by new autumn outfits and, for the girls, corsages.

The loudspeakers at the stadium were powerful enough that the pre-game announcements wafted on the wind as I set out toward campus. In the blocks between lay a goodly number of the university students' apartments. I walked, as I had before, a rambling path to the stadium, taking side streets and pausing outside old houses that were once family homes and were now divided up into student apartments. Windows were open, music blaring from inside. I'd steel myself and peek inside whenever I could, catching glimpses of disarrayed rooms with remnants of last night's party, while the tenants readied themselves for the game. Or, at other houses, they would already be gone, leaving the place to air out. The rooms were usually the same—old worn furniture and beer advertisements hung on the walls like trophies (a collegiate status symbol in the 1960s). Once in a while I would catch sight of a Playboy pinup.

Student apartments were an important factor in my college life fantasy. I'd imagine what it must be like, being away from home and living with your pals, ostensibly getting an education but also doing everything your family would never let you get away with, at *any* age. Beer blasts, college pranks, skin magazines, being able to *choose* to not go to class and there being no one to come down on you. Being able to date a girl and have a place to take her for some intimate moments, unobserved by anyone who would tell you that you were getting too close or it was "improper".

Yeah. Girls. By this time, my hormonal transformation was just about complete (premature, if you get right down to it). I started shaving years before my friends did, and when I became interested in the opposite sex, I not only did so with gusto, but I embraced a whole range of females I was interested in. High school girls. College girls. Fully matured women with cocktail dresses, mink stoles, and little white gloves. If it wore a skirt, I followed it.

And the university seemed to be crammed with more beautiful women than anywhere else. My college life fantasy, from what I observed, was not simply a fantasy for many of our students. The evidence was the occasional tousled-looking co-ed I'd see slinking guiltily from a boyfriend's apartment, having spent the night in violation of her dorm's curfew.

College girls were special then. They had a sparkle about them that you don't see much today. One side of me thinks it was just a part of the pageboy haircuts and frosted lip-gloss and go-go boots that made up the look back then. The other side of me thinks it was part of an overall virginal quality (there were considerably more virgins at that time!). Maybe both sides are right.

In any case, I leisurely walked over the hill from my neighborhood and down "fraternity row" and saw yet more beer cans on the windowsills. The sounds from the stadium became clearer and when I arrived at the gates the breeze was fairly crackling with electricity. And cigar smoke.

I don't know why, but cigar smokers always seemed to be attracted to football games like flies to garbage. There was always a surplus of them in the crowd, and to this day the smell of that smoke speaks to me of those home games of my youth. As repugnant as that smell is in other venues, it always seems strangely in place and welcome by me at sporting events.

A year or two before, I had sold programs at the games. Even after I had discontinued that largely unprofitable pastime, I still paid more attention to the crowd than to the game. It was spectacle: color cards, held by the people in one section, spelling out "WVU"; the yellow freckling of the stadium produced by thousands of chrysanthemums, worn as corsages on Homecoming Day; Band Day, with all the different schools showing their stuff at halftime. And would-be musicians in the crowd, serenading the team with those long, bugle-like plastic horns that annoyed everyone for several rows.

The wind would carry the scent of whiskey breath along with the cigar smoke. These were the days of fake binoculars with booze inside, and the hip flasks reminiscent of Prohibition days. I was, and still am, sure that the booze smuggled into the stadium tasted sweeter and stronger than that sampled in any bar or at any party.

Down on the field, cheerleaders like Susie Barnes and Dixie Downs kept the energy high. They really *led cheers* in those days. I was crazy about Dixie. I didn't know it at the time, but she was the prototype for the Negri dream girl: short, curvy, perfectly coiffed, elegantly arched eyebrows, glittering blue eyes and a sedate smile that set her apart from the other cheerleaders, who were still stick-figured and exuberant and adolescent-looking. Dixie was a *woman*, no question about it. But she was still youthful and accessible, and on the few occasions when I had been in her close proximity, she smiled so endearingly that the difference in our ages melted away (at least in my own mind). Age disparity has not bothered me a bit since.

Now I was standing in Section 17 of the stadium once more, watching her on the field and wishing that we had a date after the game. The autumn wind invigorated me and all the sights and sounds and smells colored the pictures in my head —pictures of college life, as it seemed. I couldn't wait.

I left, as I typically did, early in the third quarter and walked downtown; it was just a quarter mile away. I'd go to Walters' Newsstand first and see what was going on there, then head down to the store and eat some hot dogs. On my way, I had songs in my head I had heard earlier, coming from the radios in the dormitory and apartment windows. Those songs still sum up the whole experience and that period for me: "See You In September" by The Happenings, "Let's Hang On" by The Four Seasons, "A Lover's Concerto" by The Toys, and "Sugar and Spice" by the (never to be heard from again) Cryan Shames.

The Cryan Shames. Geez.

When I got to the City Market, everyone was listening to the game on the little radio that sat on the shelf near the peephole. The TV was off. A lot of the regulars were there. Ray Utt was on the first stool. Fred Morecraft and Wes Elkins, partners in a contracting business, were drinking beer at the other end of the bar and chatting with Grandpa. They were pleasant guys and always treated me like one of the adults—short of giving me legislative bulletins, like Hugh Runner! They greeted me when I came in.

Grandpa asked the predictable question: "D'joo eat?" I told him I hadn't and he said, "Eat something" (equally predictable). I made a couple hot dogs (the new recipe with "Frank's Red Hot" hot sauce) and went over to the last booth. Sitting there eating, I noticed something different.

The wooden back of the booth that was up against the wall, I knew, had shelves behind it. There were always the tips of advertising displays peeking up back in that corner; several dusty odds and ends were stored there. But today, a cardboard Santa Claus was peering over the back of the booth and he had not done so before. I went over to the other side of the table and looked over the top of the booth back. It was a Coca-Cola Christmas stand-up display that must have been out in the store at some point. I pulled it to one side to get a better look at it, and made a discovery. Behind it was a bottle of whiskey. I glanced over at the bar and Grandpa was reading a newspaper. I put Santa back where he had been and went back to my hot dogs.

In a few minutes, I walked behind the bar and threw my paper plate in the garbage can and heard part of a conversation between Grandpa and Fred. They were talking about some world event, evidently one that had been reported in the paper, and Grandpa was informing Fred and Wes of some fact. I couldn't follow it, any more than I understood what had been written in The Congressional Record. But Grandpa's observations must have impressed Fred, because he said to me, "Your grandfather's got so much culture, it's coming out his ears."

It was nice to have that confirmation that he was special. To me, Grandpa had always been just Grandpa but I was beginning to view him as a person with depth, with facets I might not know about. A lifetime of carrying one culture inside him while embracing another; an immigrant who didn't display any overt ethnicity, who mastered the language with hardly an accent compared to most of his countrymen. A businessman with minimal education, yet he stayed current on world events. A man who raised his children as Americans, yet himself waited until he was twenty-five before becoming a U.S. Citizen, after coming to this country at age fourteen.

The problem was that our communication style had been firmly established as superficial and brief. Most exchanges, no matter how warm and friendly, centered on who had eaten, and what he ate. Very few conversations ever dealt with complex or meaningful issues. In the first place, I had no experience talking about such things to anyone, and I am sure he had either long since given up trying to prod such things out of me, or that *he* also had no experience talking about such things. In any case, I know we felt that there was more to each other than met the eye. But the time was not right to explore it.

In a little while, I left the store to start my trek home. I thought about that mysterious bottle behind Santa Claus.

When the game was over the crowd spilled out, as it always did, into the downtown area. One look at people's faces told you whether we'd won the game or not. It didn't really matter to me. On such days, I'd sit on a wall, read the magazine I'd bought at Walters', and watch the after-game traffic jam form. Then I'd walk home for the next phase of the home game experience. Today was no different. Saturdays, even allowing for seasonal variations, were predictable. And that's just how I wanted them to be.

When I arrived home, there were several visitors crowded into the tiny kitchen, sitting around the table and all talking simultaneously. There was a bottle of whiskey on the tabletop, and I smiled inwardly when I spotted it. *What Santa Claus was that hiding behind until now?* Mom was at the kitchen sink, refilling glasses with ice.

Of the four men who sat there, two were known to me. Fred Mayhew and his son Freddie had made visits before, from Ohio. *A day for Freds*, I thought, having left Fred Morecraft at the store before walking home. Fred Mayhew Senior was a great guy and I always enjoyed seeing him. He and his son bantered more like school chums than family. They introduced me to their two friends who made the trip with them, "Blackie" and "Toesy". "Blackie" was the most reserved of the bunch. "Toesy", with his coarse looks and fat cigar, looked every bit like the enforcer who would pull the trigger if "Blackie" told him to. At least that's what I had fun pretending.

I was invited to munch on the cheese, pepperoni, and crackers laid out on several platters while Mom prepared to make spaghetti. Blackie and Freddie were discussing something that happened in the fourth quarter of the game, and Fred was telling Mom the rest of some story that I interrupted when I came in. Fred had an infectious, cackling laugh, and enjoyed his stories as much as anyone. He was laughing as he built to the conclusion of the story, with Toesy interjecting "No way." "I swear it, Toes" Fred said, grinning.

"No way, Fred."

Fred Mayhew held up his right hand as though swearing in court. "It's the gospel truth."

"No way."

"It's the gospel...MAYHEW, Mark, Luke, and John!" A tidal wave of cackling laughter. I was laughing, too, even though I didn't hear the whole story. Fred's manner was just that funny.

Noise, booze breath, and cigar smoke—it was still a home game day in the Negri kitchen!

I went downstairs to my room while everyone was in the kitchen joking. In my mind's eye, my basement bedroom was like those college apartments I'd surveyed earlier in the day. With the sounds of partying upstairs, I put on a Four Seasons record and stretched out on my bed, perfectly re-creating the feel of my college life fantasy. After a while, I felt myself melting into my bed. I drifted off to sleep, my arms wrapped around my pillow, hugging my imaginary college girlfriend. She looked like Dixie.

12

Another Saturday. I had been at the movies with several of my friends and now that we had exited the theater, the group began to disperse. I was disappointed. After cartoons, a short film, and two feature movies (plus popcorn and Junior Mints), I didn't want the fun to stop. I always wanted my gang to be more like the bands of youths we saw in the movies: cohesive, energetic, bound by some common goal, and loyal to each other.

In nearly every Bowery Boys movie, for example, when the boys got into trouble someone would yell "Okay, fellas—routine six!" And then the boys would immediately go into some perfectly timed choreography that would turn the tables on the bad guys. It seemed plausible to me (at that age) that a bunch of kids who spent a lot of time together might actually rehearse their responses to dangerous circumstances and really have a "routine six".

"Louie's Sweet Shop" in the Bowery Boys films closely resembled the layout of the City Market.

But my friends were anything but loyal and cohesive in those days, and instead of enjoying their company exploring the alleys and denizens of downtown, I was left to myself as they went their respective ways. I wanted to feel, although I didn't know how to word it at the time, kinship. Belonging. Camaraderie. And I wanted it in a familiar and interesting setting.

And all at once as I walked slowly from the Warner Theater, I realized that I was standing at the corner of Pleasant Street and that the familiar setting and comradeship I was seeking was just two blocks down the hill. At the City Market.

I walked into the store feeling like any regular. In my mind, this time, I was not the resident kid; I was a *member*. I knew all the customers by name, knew what they drank, knew their personalities. More than that. I was special. I knew all the nooks and crannies of the City Market. I was allowed in the back room; they weren't. I even knew about the bottle behind Santa Claus.

I strode up to the bar and greeted Pat Flynn. Mac was talking to Hugh Runner. Snyder was in a booth and I waved to him. He waved back heartily, like a kid from the top of a Ferris wheel. Connie was behind the bar and we gave each other dirty looks as I passed. I went into the back room and Grandma was in the kitchen tending to something in the oven. She said if I wanted a piece of pizza, I'd have to wait another ten minutes or so. I couldn't tell her what I really wanted: a beer. A beer of my own, in one of those pilsner glasses that looked so cool, right in front of me on the bar. A beer that I would sip as I would trade comments and stories with the other regulars, sitting there on a stool like all the rest of them and being a loyal City Marketeer. Yeah. That would be sweet.

But my time was not yet to be. I settled for a package of cashews, munching them casually so that I was at least consuming *something* in unison with the others. School chums Joe, Bob, Ralph, Mark, and Nickie were all my friends, sure; but these beer-sipping people were my lodge brothers, my community. I always knew where I could find them; and that, I decided, was something valuable.

Pat (far right) regales the bunch with a story.
Left to right: Ray, Grandma, and a guy named Wesley.

I moved over to where Mac and Hugh were talking, and heard Mac talking about the shutters he bought for his house. Pat shouted from the other end of the bar. "Are you talking about those damn shutters again?"

Mac looked over in his direction, not annoyed in the least. "Well, I got a terrific deal on them," he said. Hugh made some comments about their adding to the property values, and Mac told some rambling story about hiring the men to install them. Something about how he had to wait, but now there were on and they just transformed the building. He turned his attention to me. "I got them for *all* the windows, too" he said. "You should come look at them." I said I might. I moved slowly toward the other end. The man next to Mac turned his head in his direction and Mac said, "They have louvers! I got a great deal on them!" The man quickly turned his head back to the TV set. After a quick survey of faces in the room, I deduced that Mac had been talking about his shutters not only that whole day but probably for the past week.

When I left the store that day, I stopped in the middle of the block and reversed direction. I knew where Mac lived, just two and a half blocks away. It wasn't far out of my way to walk past his house and check out the shutters on the way home.

His house was an old one, one of those 1800s non-descript rectangles with a pitched roof. A small storefront had been built onto the front at some point. Mac had operated an appliance repair shop there for years. There was no business in there now, though. Just the distinctive look of the only building to border the small bridge that spanned Decker's Creek, just above where it drained into the river. The distinctive look that was enhanced, I now saw, by black shutters that were only two-thirds the length of the windows they graced. I looked at them, stunned, and then pictured the comical little man with barely a chin and a large Adam's apple, stopping to admire them each day as he left home. I couldn't stop laughing. All the way home I thought about the phrase "I got a terrific deal on them."

I stopped at Ralph's house on the way home and told him the story of Mac's shutters. He was going to his grandmother's house in that same neighborhood later. He'd look for them, he said. We sat on his front steps for a little while and then I remembered I never got that piece of pizza at the store. "Wanna eat some meatballs?"

"Sure," Ralph said. We went to my house where Mom had already completed the weekly sauce ritual. The week's supply of spaghetti sauce was begun Friday night, with the browning of the meatballs and the initial making of the sauce. It cooked for a while that night, then she would cook it again for a few hours on Saturday, becoming thicker and more flavorful as time passed. It was typical to have a bowl of meatballs and the not-quite-finished sauce on Saturday, dipping bread into its medium redness. It started out bright red on Friday, was medium on Saturday, and dark for Sunday dinner. Ralph, whose only known ethnic connection was a distant trace of Cherokee, learned to love those meatballs like a real Italian.

Mom poured iced tea for the two of us and said, "Ralph, you sit here. Connie's bringing Grandpa home soon." We were halfway through our bowls when Grandpa came in the front door. He took off his hat, regarded us eating, and set about getting himself a bowl of the meatballs and sauce also. Ralph shot me a glance, smiling. I knew what he was thinking. He was waiting to see what Grandpa would say, since he couldn't say "D'joo eat?" But Grandpa just said "Hi" and sat down.

A few minutes went by and Mom was looking toward the front door. "Did Connie come in?" she asked me. I said she had not, and Mom said, "She's taking a long time to park the car." She stood there for a few more minutes, then said, in a louder voice, "Daddy, where's Connie?"

I waited for him to say "Huh?" but he didn't. Barely looking up from his meal, Grandpa made the matter-of-fact statement "She's up at the collision." He pronounced it *co-LEE-shun*.

"Collision? What collision?!" Mom answered, and started for the door. Ralph and I looked at each other and back at Grandpa, who was unconcerned and engrossed in his dinner. We both snickered and headed for the door also.

From the sidewalk we all saw Connie's car and another car in what might poetically be called an embrace, up the hill at an intersection where she was turning around and hit an oncoming vehicle in the process. The occupants of the other car were standing in front, talking to Connie and surveying the damage.

Ralph and I went back in, finished our bowls, and took our iced teas out to the front porch. We sat on the glider, laughing in waves at how downplayed the whole affair was in Grandpa's eyes. He wasn't going to waste time up at the co-lee-shun. He walked down the street and started having dinner as though nothing had happened. "Oh, she's up at the co-lee-shun!" Ralph mimicked. At the height of our laughing, Connie stepped up to the porch, which only increased the humor. Ralph was practically wheezing with laughter. Connie was livid. She glared at us and went inside.

In a little while, Ralph left to go to his grandmother's house, and I descended the basement steps to my bedroom. Time to hide from the world, and especially Connie. I killed time until the late movie, which was a weekly ritual.

Saturday night was, as always, crowned by watching Chiller Theater. Every week, a double feature of suspense, classic horror, or just plain silliness (Mexican masked wrestler/ superhero fights zombie safecrackers) of which I never tired.

There had been a party going on in the house behind ours for some time. Most of the houses in the neighborhood had college student apartments, and this kind of weekend activity was common. I could tell from the voices that the party had expanded into the yard that bordered our back yard.

The second movie started about 1:30 a.m. and I realized that the music and sounds of talking had suddenly ceased. Then I noticed a rhythmic glowing behind the roller blind of the window next to the television. There in the dark room, a pinkish light showed itself behind the blind, then disappeared, then returned, over and over. I got curious and pulled the blind aside to see a police car stopped on the street behind, its flashing red light painting my blind. The loud music had been abruptly stopped when someone spotted the cruiser. Where did everyone go? The party must have been filled with underage drinkers.

I saw the policeman now. He was standing on the sidewalk, fanning a flashlight beam across the yard. He made several passes and I watched with interest. This was better than the movie! I thought I saw something move on our side of the wire fence that separated the properties, and when the cop made another pass with his beam, I saw the outlines of several people in our yard, crouched behind Grandma's peony bush. He couldn't see them, however, and finally left. The people stayed crouched behind the bush for the longest time. They must have jumped the fence in their panic when they caught sight of the police cruiser. Funny.

The next morning I got curious as to whether they had bent any of the fence during their climbing, so I went out to the back yard. The old wire fence was intact. I looked across into their yard and there were cups and paper plates strewn about. Then my foot found something. There, under the peonies, was a bottle. A nearly full bottle of something called Southern Comfort.

I took it inside my bedroom and had a taste. Pretty darn good! I had tasted bourbon before and liked it, but this was different somehow. Its sweet taste was, in retrospect, the perfect starter liquor for a teenager (if such a thing deserves to exist). I hid the bottle, realizing at once that I was now joined in crime with Grandpa. There was a cosmic connection between the bottle behind the Santa Claus display at the City Market and the bottle I would conceal behind a panel in my bedroom. I would mentally name this category "Hidden Pleasures", and in the years since have come to realize that the men in my family are happiest when they are enjoying something that is completely their own, away from all other eyes.

13

Grandpa's health declined in his seventies, and he had more "sieges" of gout and heart trouble. Connie began helping out at the store more. What effect this had on business I could only guess, but there was ample evidence that the customers at the City Market regarded her in the same way as old Max Weintrob the tailor had described her—crabby.

I was there at the store one evening, experiencing the minor thrill of being asked to make a couple hot dogs for a customer. As I ladled the chili onto them, I heard a man ask Connie if I played any sports. "No," she said, "He's the bookworm type." How I hated this kind of conversation.

Someone appeared in the corner of my eye, returning from the men's room. Oh boy! Mac is here! Connie glanced over at him and made her disgusted face. "He's been driving me crazy," she said to me. I could feel a snicker building up.

Mac saw me and got his bottle of beer and came over to the bar. He was obviously tipsy. *Inebriato*, I thought, with a sense of pride that I could both diagnose the condition and also express it in Italian. Mac started a conversation interspersed with giggles, as I had experienced before, and I knew I was in for some entertainment. I was trying to figure out what he was talking about, but Connie started yelling at him to sit back down. He looked at her, then back at me, and grinned. He resumed his giggly monologue and I was chuckling because not only was he such a comical-looking character, he seemed to really enjoy trying Connie's patience to the limit.

Another outburst from Connie brought Grandma out from the kitchen. "Mom," she said like a little kid complaining about a sibling, "He won't stop!" I almost expected her to stamp her feet on the floor. Mac just laughed and leaned closer to talk to me.

"All right, you," Grandma said as she came around to the front of the bar. She put her hands on his back and started pushing him away. Mac giggled. I giggled. She pointed him in the direction of the door and played bulldozer. As he passed me he said, barely able to control his laughter, "Sh-she keeps her money in the sugar bowl!" He said it looking at Connie, and I burst into laughter. Grandma pushed him the entire length of the store and out the door. *She keeps her money in the sugar bowl.* What a wonderfully nonsensical statement to make me laugh and make Connie mad. Now *this* was a good time.

I had told Grandma that I'd go to play bingo with her that night, and it was now time to go. Connie would just have to stew there in the store without any more backup tonight. She still looked rattled from Mac as we left. Funny as hell.

The bingo game was at the Knights of Columbus hall, right around the corner from the store. She gathered up her things and we walked to the "K of C". Unlike the Moose Club or the Eagles Lodge, where I'd gone to bingo games with her before, the game room was in the basement. At all the other places, it had been on an upper floor. I liked the K of C. We found a place on opposite sides of a long cafeteria table and settled in. We placed our cards on the tabletop, and put markers in the all the middle "free" spaces. Why was there a free space? I asked once, but no one knew.

"B eight!" the caller said through the public address system. All the people scanned their cards for the number in the first column.

Grandma would play many bingo cards at once. I could play at most four. She had a quick eye, and the cards were spread across some distance on the table in front of her. She had her reference astrology and number books at her side, and at the top of the centermost bingo card, she placed Bruno. Bruno was a little statue of a bear, and he was her luck charm. He was accompanied by several four-leaf clovers, which Grandma had found and Scotch-taped to pieces of cardboard. Homemade, plus mass-produced, luck charms insured that no efforts were overlooked in trying to influence a game of chance.

Maybe because of the artwork in *Zolar's All-Star Dream Book* or because of the Near East images associated with occultism in the earlier part of the 20th Century, I felt like I was doing my part by drinking Royal Crown cola. The bottle had a depiction of the pyramids on it. I would get lost in that image, thinking about the mysteries of ancient Egypt, of braziers burning incense, of Western men in tuxedos wearing turbans who had traveled in the lands of mystery and were now applying their mastery of ancient mystical arts.

It was thrilling enough a fantasy that I was able to ignore the fact that the "incense" here was cigarette smoke, that the few men who came to the game never wore a tuxedo in their lives (much less a turban), and the only ancient mystery was how people continued to play games where the house always made more money than the players ever won.

Still, it was sort of exciting to be there, trying to influence the fall of the numbered balls in the moderator's drum with my mental powers. After all, I was drinking RC, with the pyramid on the bottle! Grandma didn't presume to have any powers herself. That's what Bruno was for.

"N thirty-three!"

I looked around the room. The woman from the City Market was there with her husband and boyfriend. I spotted another familiar face, a woman who worked for an old lawyer. She pushed him around town in his wheelchair and I saw them often. Her name was Hazel. On her night off, she played bingo like many of the others. She was slight, slumped, and balding on top. The hair she did have was always unkempt, yet—curiously—was dyed the same color as her name. I probably didn't know the word *incongruous* yet, but I had already developed an eye for those things that logically should not co-exist. *Why would someone not brush her hair and yet dye the gray?* She looked up suddenly as I was staring at her pink scalp and I looked away. Maybe the RC Cola and the other artifacts of the mystic East had amplified my brainpower after all.

"G fifty-four!"

Oh shoot! I had B8 and didn't realize it. I grabbed a marker and put it on the square.

"O sixty- SAVun," the woman called out. *Sav-un*, I thought. *Sixty SAV-un. Who talks like that? And why?* Interspersed between the regular games, there were special games that were played on little paper cards that were passed out to whomever wanted to play for higher stakes. These "special" games were always pronounced "SPAY-shul" by the announcer.

"Bingo!" someone cried out. There was a murmur of disappointment throughout the room. I curtailed my internal analysis of the local dialect.

Grandma won a couple games this night. I had won once in the past. I was under orders to quickly tell her if I got bingo, because a minor wasn't allowed to win any money. On that occasion, she called out "Bingo!" and slid my card over to her side to wait for the woman to come over and check the numbers.

After I played bingo, I always felt like I had taken one of those national, standardized tests we sometimes had in school. My brain got tired having to pay ruthless attention to those numbers for so long a time. The dozens of old ladies with their cigarettes and their low, droning conversations didn't seem to have any problem keeping track, no matter how infirm, slow, or depleted by alcohol they were.

During the specials that I declined to play, I sketched some of the characters from the City Market on pieces of scrap paper. This kept me entertained and lessened the chances of my missing a number and losing a game for Grandma. I resolved to keep at it until I could draw Mac perfectly.

Mom picked us up after the games were over, and we were home in a couple minutes. Grandpa had eaten and was going to bed. Connie was doing her lint-picking routine, sighing and clucking her tongue as she bent over the throw rug, blocking my way into the kitchen. Mom was running water into the sink.

"Leave the dishes, I'll do them," Connie said, straightening up. Mom turned around and looked daggers at Connie.

"What?" Connie said, with a challenging tone. Mom just kept staring at her until her point was driven home, whatever it was. I guessed what the unspoken words would have been. *Oh, you will? WHEN will you? Tomorrow?* Mom turned back around to the sink and started washing a plate.

Tsk! Connie clucked. She stood there for another minute glaring in Mom's direction, then turned and went upstairs.

Watching them have these tense moments was like watching two animals staring each other down in the wild, each waiting for the other one to expose its throat.

Connie left me alone when Mom was around, but—like a competitive sibling—was eager to start trouble when we were alone. The next day was a good example.

Ralph and I were going to some event and I was getting ready to go when Connie picked a fight about something. I don't recall the subject now; there were so many over the years. But I had a convenient way to get out of it when Ralph knocked on the front door. I walked away, went downstairs, let Ralph in, and went to get my coat. He sat down on the couch in the living room. I came back into the room and Connie had come downstairs to renew the argument. Somewhere in the ridiculous framework of the fight, she used the word February. She pronounced it (as many people do) as *Feb-yoo-ary*. She had my dander up now, and I was not only aggravated by her incessant fight picking but I had also had a bellyful of bad English the night before at bingo. Mispronouncing February was the equivalent of the other animal exposing its throat. I decided to pounce.

"It's not feb-yoo-ary, it's feb-ROO-ary" I said.

"Feb-yoo-ary," she said, indignantly.

""Feb-ROO-ary!" I countered.

She turned up her volume. "Don't be ridiculous! It's feb-YOO-ary!" she said. "Feb! Yoo! Ary!"

I turned and pointed to a calendar on the wall. I placed my finger on the second month, smiled smugly, and said, "What's the fourth letter in that word?"

I wish I could have a videotape of this because the scowl never left her face, but she blinked twice and there was a subtle change in her expression as the realization sank in. The other animal was frozen in her tracks now, unable to withstand the claws and fangs of the awesome beast in front of her, and with her back to a cliff. I smiled wickedly.

I pressed the attack. "What's that letter?!"

She blinked again. Then, the most bizarre strategy I have ever witnessed unfolded.

"Well, anyway," she said, "it's not feb-roo-ary…it's *feber-yooARY!*"

Feber-yoo-ary? Ralph broke into uncontrollable laughter. Connie stood in the same spot without moving, except to regard Ralph for a moment and then looked back at me but didn't say anything. Ralph had collapsed on the couch, hammering his fist into the throw cushion in his hilarity. I was starting to break up myself, despite trying not to. Connie finally turned and went back upstairs.

Outside, Ralph was still laughing about *feber-yoo-ary*. "Your family's nuts," he said. It wasn't the first time I would hear that from him.

The irrepressible Ralph

14

My buddy Nicky was with me when I stopped in at the store one afternoon. Grandma asked me to take a package down to Helen the Greek Woman. No matter how many times I was exposed to this person, Grandma always referred to her that way. It was a title of sorts, almost a one-word name: *Helenthegreekwoman.*

"Taste this, it was made by Helen the Greek Woman."

"I went to bingo with Helen the Greek Woman."

She gave me the bundle to take to Helen the Greek Woman, and as I started for the door, Nicky spied Mac sitting in a booth and went over to him.

"Hey, are you Danny McMillen's grandfather?" Nicky asked him. I saw Mac's face brighten and he nodded his head. Nicky drew closer to the booth and as he did, I saw Grandma's face. She had a look of mixed alarm and disapproval. She shook her head rapidly, as if to say "No, don't!"

It was too late. Nicky was in a conversation with the funny guy, telling him where he went to school and where his desk was in relation to Mac's grandson's, etc. Mac asked him a few questions, and I intervened and said we had to go. I was chuckling to myself as we left, and Nicky was continuing his conversation about his classmate.

"Yeah, Danny's grandfather's got a lot of money, boy."

"Mac? Rich? That can't be," I said.

"No, it's true. Danny told me."

This just seemed inconceivable. I didn't have that long to think about it, though, because Helen the Greek Woman's place was only a block away and we were already there. Helen and her husband operated a small restaurant next to the bus station that had been there since the '30s. Its fading signage still said "The Lamont Sandwich Shop", but I never heard anyone call it by that name. And certainly not by anyone in my family. It was Helen the Greek Woman's.

The old place had changed little over the years. There were a few booths in the front windows. Six stools stood at the counter. Behind the counter, several magazines and comic books were displayed on a length of clothesline, attached with wooden clothespins—a method of exhibiting merchandise that was common thirty years earlier but was now extinct, except for here. A glass-covered dish of pie was on the counter. The shiny enamel paint on the walls was two-tone: a yellowing cream color and a darker, mustard hue on the lower four feet of wall, down to the floor. There was the slightly sweet smell of hot grill and oil in the air. One could easily imagine it was the 1930s, and fedora-wearing passengers would exit the Greyhound next door and get a sandwich and a cup of coffee in here.

Helen greeted us from behind the counter and I gave her the package from Grandma. She was short and fleshy, had salt-and-pepper hair that was done up in a beehive, and a little wart on her chin. She wore a pink apron with little flowers on it. I introduced her to my friend Nicky. "Ooo, you gots the same name as my hoos-band! Hey Nick!" She called out over her shoulder. Nick emerged from the other side of the curtain to the kitchen. He was a friendly little man with gray hair and laughing eyes, and I always enjoyed him.

They offered us something to drink, and we accepted. We had a conversation I was enjoying but Nicky was getting antsy. I wished I could stay. Nick the Greek Man was talking about the street and the hotels that used to be on that block back in the old days, and how the cars would be lined up and parked all the way to the corner—which was unbelievable, because the street was now a major thoroughfare. I couldn't even imagine parking had existed.

"Yeah," Nick said, "All the boot lickers would come across the bridge from Westover and come down here." I waited for more information to make better sense of what he was telling me, but the topic quickly changed and Helen gave me a message to give to Grandma. Nicky and I said our goodbyes and backtracked to the City Market. On the way, I realized what Nick had been talking about. *Bootleggers*. Not boot lickers.

Later that evening, after Nicky and I had parted and I went home, I asked Grandma about Mac.

"Nicky said Mac is rich. He isn't, is he?"

"Oh, he made a lot of money in the stock market."

I was amazed. "You mean he really does have money?!"

"Uh huh," she said, as she minced some garlic and tossed it into a pot. That was all she had to say about it. She seemed put out about something, so I didn't press the conversation.

I thought to myself: *The stock market. That's something to do with playing numbers, right?* It would be a few years before history class would give me a better idea of how economics works. But I was to receive my first lesson in financial realities later that week.

Mom dropped the bombshell. "We might have to close the store."

"Why?" I asked, aghast at the idea.

"Grandma and Grandpa can't pay to renew the beer license."

I couldn't understand how one purchase would be both so critical and such a hurdle. It wasn't a huge amount of money, but apparently the store just barely paid the expenses month after month, and when the yearly fee came due there was nothing extra set aside. I asked for a better picture of the situation, and Mom said, "Grandpa never saved money." Then she told me the story of his stomach operation, and the money crunch that arose over that.

And yet I remembered an old friend of Mom's talking about when they were in high school in the '30s and how Grandpa's expensive cream-colored Buick was the talk of the town. I remembered Mom mentioning that Grandpa used to rent a garage to park the car. I recalled pictures of Grandpa in nice, three-piece suits from that time, and the pictures of Grandma on vacation at Atlantic City. But all that was in the days of the original City Market. Before Skid Row.

Mom reiterated. "Grandpa never saved money."

I was depressed for days. I was in high school by this time, which was not as much fun as it should have been in the first place, and now I had a worry that really ate at me. I stared out the window during class and felt panic for the first time in my life. The City Market had always been there. It was the glue that held the various components of the Negri family together and now someone was telling me it wasn't going to be there?

I spent a lot of time confronting the idea that somebody's goofy, boozy grandfather, with his shutters that didn't fit his windows, had money while my grandfather "with culture coming out his ears" had nothing.

Time passed and the store was still open. No one ever talked about it to me, but I imagine Mom took out a loan to pay for the beer license.

"You've had too much," Grandma says to a City Marketeer.

15

It was my senior year of high school. Plans were being made for the Senior Class trip to New York City. I thought of the wondrous skyline, the concentration of so many of the places I always wanted to see, the ultimate urban destination! It was an exciting prospect. I also thought: *Hmmm. My Dad's there. Maybe I could kill two birds with one stone.* I was increasingly interested in the man who wrote me those periodic letters with their gentle wit. Most recently he had sent me a record album from a stint he did in New Orleans with a road company. They were doing a play there and he thought I would be interested in recordings of authentic jazz (so authentic, in fact, that they spelled it *jass* on the record). It was a departure from the music I had been listening to; after a few times, though, the record appealed to me. Without phrasing it as such, I thought that this jazz probably captured something of my father as much as it had New Orleans.

But I had another plot developing in my head. I had become increasingly interested in my Italian heritage, and wanted to visit the old hometown of Collelongo, see my aunts there. Grandpa's sisters wrote letters every once in a while during the time I was growing up, and now I was curious to see where everything came from.

I proposed to Mom that she put the money for my class trip into a fund for me to later visit Italy. I would gladly forego even a trip to New York City in order to visit our ancestral home. To my surprise, she agreed.

All my classmates were making plans for the New York City trip, and I got an unexpected reaction when I announced I was not going along. They didn't believe me.

"Ha ha! SURE he's going to Italy!" I don't know what they thought was the real reason I would opt out of the class trip, but I resented the treatment, just as I resented the hundreds of other insults I endured during four years of the cliquish parochial school. *High school is ending the same way it began*, I thought.

My friends came back from the New York trip with funny stories and wonderful memories and I had to shore myself up internally by reminding myself that I was going to Italy. Yet I still felt bad for missing out on this adventure; but it was my choice. I was taunted again for not going. Then before long graduation day arrived, and I unexpectedly felt the same panic as I had when told that the store might close. I really didn't like school but it was all that I knew. What was I going to do without this regular routine and familiar place? I had a small number of school friends. Was I really not going to see them on a regular basis again? Some of them I had seen every day since first grade.

I was extremely anxious at the post-graduation banquet. My classmates sat with their attending relatives in clusters at long cafeteria tables. Everyone, parents included, just hunkered down to shovel in the free food and I didn't see anyone interacting. Mom and I sat together at the end of one of the tables, side by side, and no one around us was making conversation. *We* weren't even making conversation. Feeling like I was missing a party, I got up and walked around to my various friends' stations, made a few wisecracks about the nuns finally letting us out; I said hello to their parents, shook the outstretched hands of their fathers. Each one barely paused in the rush to devour the dinner.

Having the memory of the Café 422 and the warm and festive atmosphere created by Grandpa's countrymen, who hopped from table to table and were so entertaining and engaging—I somehow expected to take my place beside whomever their counterparts were at this time and place. Salutations should be made! Glasses should be raised! But it was not to be. There might have been Italians in the room, but they weren't *my* kind of Italians.

My attempts to inject a party atmosphere failed, I circled back to my seat, with Mom glowering at me. She was silent for the rest of the time we were there, which was not long. In true parochial school style, everyone rose and started filing out the door, as though the school bell had rung.

Once in the car, Mom was furious. "You wouldn't even *sit* with me!" she fumed. "How do you think that looked to everybody?"

I sat in the back seat, angry and disappointed, and in a total panic about the future. She would not speak to me the rest of the day. I recall not sleeping that night.

The summer passed without event until the time drew near for college registration. I wanted to study criminology but Mom was of no help in my finding out which classes I needed for that pursuit. She was dead set on my getting a journalism degree (like her), and we clashed. It was not something she cared to debate. On the night before I was to register for classes, I experienced dread like I had never felt before. All my former fears were now reduced to trivialities: forgotten school projects; unfinished homework on a Sunday night; fear of being turned down for a date with the girl you had a crush on. Those were nothing. This was dread with a capital D.

I ascended the stairs to her bedroom and confessed my anxiety. It took a lot to do it; we had grown adversarial over the past few years and I was admitting, *exposing*, my insecurity and the fact that my teenage wisdom and experience might actually be insufficient. My cocksure attitude was gone and my soul was laid bare, but it did no good. She wouldn't discuss it. There would be no indulgence, no guidance, certainly no sympathy. Served me right for waiting until the last minute to express myself.

The next morning, I became a journalism major.

My entry year of college, I found, was nothing like my earlier fantasies formed by walking around the stadium and fraternity houses. First of all, I had to live at home. So the images of student apartments and their non-stop socializing atmosphere vaporized pretty quickly. Although my bedroom was in the basement of the house and had a separate entrance, it was far from private. Once, I brought a girl I had dated in high school back to my room on a Friday afternoon after our last classes. Mom discovered it and hit the roof.

Secondly, most of the classes I was taking other than journalism classes seemed to have no pertinence and certainly no innate capacity to help keep one's eyes open. There was political science, psychology, physical education, and geology. I don't recall how that geology class got in there, but my father had graduated from this very university with a geology degree and that sort of underscored my bewilderment as I realized that he was never employed in any phase of the geological field.

If my mother with a journalism degree became a secretary, and my father with a geology degree became an actor, what the hell am I doing? The thought occurred to me often, but not more than three or four times a day.

One elective course that I chose, though, almost made all the other mind-numbing class work worthwhile. I took Italian for my language requirement.

Here was knowledge not just for its own sake but a pursuit that was as practical as it was enjoyable. I came to the happy realization that language learning was totally unlike other subjects. With my other classes, you might accumulate knowledge that you would eventually demonstrate by examination, which would lead to a degree, which would lead to employment in that field, and with further effort and time you might excel in that field, etc. But mastering a language gave you growing skill day by day. Not only was it of practical value, its worth was not deferred until the final exam or degree. If you fouled up the final exam, all your conversational ability didn't disappear! And I wasn't doing this to get a job with Berlitz. This was highly personal. I still intended to go visit my aunts in Italy.

Grandpa, of course, was delighted that I was taking Italian. By this time he was somewhat infirm and didn't leave the house. So I would see him when I came home between classes. I would read my Italian lessons for him and he complimented me on my naturalistic way of speaking. I told him that the instructor in language lab had also complimented me. While listening to the tape and repeating the phrases, I found another voice cutting in on my headphones. He asked, "Is Italian your first language?" I replied in the negative and he said, "Well, you have a hell of an accent."

"I never taught Eleanor and Connie the language when they were little. I should have," Grandpa said.

"Why didn't you?" I asked.

"They were Americans." He looked away, toward the opposite wall, and I couldn't tell if he was staring out the living room window or through a window of time.

Saluti !

16

I got word from my other Grandma that my father was appearing here and there on episodes of the daytime soap opera *All My Children.* I made sure I was home for the episode he was supposed to be in, but after watching the whole show, he had never appeared. The next week, though, he was on and I caught it. There he was, my vaguely remembered progenitor, playing a bartender in a brief appearance. A bartender! His patrons were prosperous and well dressed, a world away from the City Market regulars.

I thought about how I used to watch soap operas with Grandma when I was young, before I was in school. Now I felt that I, like my father, was *in* one.

As my collegiate life rolled on, I had an increasing number of intimate conversations with Grandpa, which contrasted with an increasing number of *hostile* ones with Mom. Life was strange. I didn't see any of my old high school friends, some of whom I had known since first grade. Ralph's uncle found him a job in Maryland and he moved there. The old neighborhood seemed different. The two positive forces for me then were Grandpa and my Italian professor. My dad was just a face on a TV show. I didn't know it at the time, but I was at an age where male mentorship was very important, and I was only just starting to realize what had been missing in my life as I was growing up.

"Why did we come here, Grandpa?"

"We didn't have anything back in the old country."

"No," I said, "Why come *here*?"

"Oh, it was virgin territory."

I thought about the historical photographs of the region I had seen, how most of the sights I was used to were not yet in evidence. There was definitely an undeveloped look to the area in those photos of the time when Grandpa and his father were struggling immigrants.

Beneath my basement "apartment" (bedroom and kitchen but no bathroom) lay an underground room hewn out of the foundation of the house by my great-grandfather. It was there that he made his wine, and I began spending more time down there, prying open the old trap door under the stairs and descending into the cave-like atmosphere and feeling connected to those days when it was "virgin territory".

One day while sorting through the old forgotten odds and ends stored in the wine cellar and long forgotten, I found a dusty, tarnished *thing* that I recognized from one of the old family photos. When Grandpa was young, he played the baritone horn in the Morgantown Italian-American Band. There was a picture of him posing in a photographer's studio, wearing his band uniform and embracing his horn, which was standing upright beside him. They looked like two friends, encouraged by the photographer to "stand closer".

I decided that I would clean up the old thing, find the right kind of metal polish, and surprise Grandpa with it for his birthday. He always lamented that everything related to his youth had been thrown away. Yes, this would be a worthy project.

But personal projects, particularly creative projects, received more of my attention than my studies. Though I liked it, I didn't really push myself in my Italian classes, but I did all right due to just having an ear for the language. I couldn't say the same for my other classes. My grades were terrible,. I was dissatisfied with what I was doing; Mom was dissatisfied with *how* I was doing. There were other things I wanted to learn, truly wanted to learn, and they had nothing to do with the lineup I was forced to take. I proposed that I drop a few classes (notably Political Science and the dreaded 8 a.m. Geology!) and improve my grades in the others, adding some classes I wanted to take. Mom would have none of it. The gap between what I wanted and what she wanted *for me* revealed itself to be far wider than I had thought. A number of fights about it resulted in her demanding that I drop my beloved Italian class. I was still living at home, she was still the boss, and I reluctantly went to tell my professor that I would not be in his classroom anymore.

Maybe it was an instant realization, or maybe because of my recently developing a dialogue with Grandpa, I had a sudden clarity about my need for a male mentor. I was no sooner sitting down in my professor's office than I was baring my soul to him. He was the only faculty member I had connected with, and—perhaps because he was of Mediterranean blood—he felt like family. The poor guy sat helpless as I spilled my guts to him and was flattered that his class was the only one that meant anything to me. He was encouraging, and convinced me that it was not the end, and that I would wind up in his classroom once again, after I worked out what I was going to do.

"*Corragio*, my friend," he said as he clapped me on the shoulder. "*Corragio*."

Walking through campus that day I felt anything but courageous. I was soggy-eyed and snotty-nosed and my future was a question mark. But as I walked home, a new strength was growing in me. It is a constant for me that I only leap to action and do something new or significant when I have been angered. Now I was angry. I resented my mother's domination, I thought about the trip to Italy that had never come off, and I especially remembered the taunting I got for not going on the class trip. "I got robbed of New York *and* Italy," I said to myself. "Now I'm wasting the money that would have taken me to those places, by taking classes that have nothing to do with anything. My money. *My* money!" I thought.

I considered the glass bank that had sat on top of my mother's dresser all the time I was growing up. Money I got for birthdays and Christmas often went into the "college fund". By the time I reached home that day, I had hatched a plot that made me smile.

The "college fund" money had been put into a joint checking account with Mom's and my names on it, for me to write checks for textbooks, fees, etc. She held the checkbook, however; I had to write out those checks in her presence.

I decided to get my money back.

I searched around when Mom was not at home, but could never find the checkbook. *All I need is one check*! I looked everywhere. She apparently carried that with her, night and day. Then, suddenly, the solution came to me. I went to the bank and ordered a new checkbook filler for the account. The teller brought me the new set of checks. I tore one off, dumped the rest in the waste can, and wrote out a check for the full balance of the "college fund". I deposited it into my personal account that I held since winning the football pool at twelve years old. I walked out of the First National Bank building with a look on my face that must have been a mix of grim determination and smug satisfaction. I was John Dillinger and Ocean's Eleven rolled into one. I had pulled off a slick heist and now I was going to top that achievement.

One block away was a travel service. I entered and made arrangements for that trip to Italy I had been denied.

One block farther down was the post office. I applied for my passport there.

Once home, I wrote a letter to my aunts to tell them that I was coming for a visit. Writing in Italian was like writing in code, for although she wasn't going to see the letter, it was a thrill for me that my mother wouldn't be able to read it if she did. I opened up the secret bar in my room and made myself a celebratory drink. It had been a busy day.

A few weeks went by, and I had my passport. My aunts had written, welcoming me, and the date was set. I picked up my tickets at the travel agency. I got home in the late afternoon, and I heard Mom get home earlier than usual. From all the years living in the basement and hearing the staccato of her high heels on the floors above, I was like a jungle native who can tell you what the drums are saying. Today, the drums weren't saying anything good. I could tell that her pace was faster than usual, and she didn't stop off at any of the usual spots in the house. She headed right for the basement door.

The door flew open and she came stomping down the stairs to my room. There was no mistaking it. She was on the warpath. She had a piece of paper in her hand; it was the monthly bank statement.

"What is the meaning of this?!" she screamed. Although there was some adrenalin going as there always was in these altercations, I was essentially calm and confident. I explained in a matter-of-fact voice that I was flying to Italy in a couple weeks as per our agreement when I was in high school. I don't recall much of anything she said in her tirade; it was like watching a TV with the sound turned off. I was completely in my own world. I remember even today how delicious it felt that I was finally in the driver's seat for the first time in my life. I was smiling. The more I smiled, the madder she got. I didn't hear her. It was a "done deal". There was nothing she could do. There was nothing she could take away anymore.

Whether they came from comic books or from respectable literature, a number of corny phrases issued from my mouth from time to time when I felt the occasion to be momentous. That night, I said aloud, "I am the master of my fate." It was probably the only time in my life where I had felt that to be true. I reviewed all its variations. *I* am the master of my fate. I *am* the master of my fate. I am the master of my *fate*.

One thing was for sure. Life wasn't going to be the same much longer.

17

I was home one afternoon when a telegram came for me. Connie was upstairs and had signed for it. She opened the door to the basement and yelled down. "It's from Aunt Giulia," she said, revealing that she had opened my mail.

"Give it to me," I said.

She ignored the request and stood at the top of the stairs reading the message. "It says here that she will be at... what's that name?" She screwed up her face. "Something... airport."

"Give me my telegram!" I yelled as I started up the steps toward her.

"It says 'will meet Jove'...did you use the name 'Jove' when you wrote to them?"

"What? Gimme that." I snatched at the paper but she pulled away. I got it on my second try. A litany of screamed complaints and accusations, most of which I had heard countless times, ran out of her mouth in a torrent. The bratty kid in her had emerged, and was not going to stop yelling until she got her way. I wasn't about to give it to her. I shut the door and descended the steps to my room, only to hear her open the door again and continue the screaming. I made for the street door and went outside. It was chilly. I waited until I was down the street before I allowed myself the pleasure of sitting down and reading my own mail. I sat on the cold wall outside Ralph's old house and looked at the telegram. It was the only one I had ever received. There was the message. It read: WILL BE MEETING JOV FEBRUARY 8 AT FIUMICINO AIRPORT.

It took me only a second to realize that some human or technical foible between Europe and the U.S. had transformed "you" into "jov". But not Connie. She had to concoct an alias for me. According to her, I was telling my own aunts my name was really "Jove"! I would have laughed if I hadn't still been under an adrenaline rush from yet another fight in the Negri house. Then I looked at the next word. Connie had deliberately skipped over the word "February" when she was reading it out loud. I wondered how she would have pronounced it if she hadn't omitted it. I thought of Ralph, and then I laughed after all.

Feber-uary. By Jove! I wish Ralph was here.

In a week, "Jove" was on his way. Without ever once stepping into an airplane before, I crossed the Atlantic in a Boeing 747, which was then a new and almost impossibly big craft. I was amazed with the entire thing: the sights, the smells, the technology, the people. Having once had a fear of heights, I had either left that behind or was cured permanently by the magnificent view of the land receding until we were covered by clouds. Then, my first vision of the world above the clouds. How could it be so blue? Bluer than the bluest sky of the fairest day described in the lyrics of the happiest love song. That kind of blue. I loved it. Down below, somewhere, women were screaming and arguing. It didn't matter if it had anything to do with me. I couldn't hear it. I was going places. I was master of my fate.

The eight-hour flight went quickly; so quickly, in fact, that I was almost disappointed to land. I was enjoying the views, the socializing with other passengers, the drinks, even the meals. And most of all, the inaccessibility. No one can come stomping down the steps uninvited when you're relaxing on a 747. Don't feel like talking? Put your headphones on and listen to some music. Six channels.

But land we did, and I found my aunts waiting at the exit for me. I hadn't really thought things through as far as I should have—how were complete strangers going to find each other in a major international airport? But I wasn't worried after I looked over in one direction and saw two old women standing with a man, and one of the women looked like Grandpa! It was Aunt Giulia, all right. She and Aunt Felicetta clamped onto me as though I was going to float away, and after being smothered in kisses, I found myself in a car leaving Rome and heading for Collelongo, the family home.

On the ride, Aunt Giulia asked about my life and how Grandpa was, and the store. I told them about all of these things, using my most fluid Italian, and I remember feeling very gratified that I was not nervous speaking the language as I thought I might have been. I could even remember most of the words I wanted to use without slipping into French, which I had taken in high school. Often in Italian class, the French word would appear when I was trying to remember the Italian word for something.

Aunt Felicetta was not as outgoing as Aunt Giulia, but then she spoke up.

"*Perche non studio l'Italiano?*" she asked. Why didn't I study Italian?

I had one of those "weird dream" moments. It was the kind of thing that happens in a weird dream, after all—you have been speaking a language to someone and then they ask you *in that language* why you can't speak it. As if none of the previous conversation had taken place.

I replied that I was taking Italian at the university. I really wasn't able to think of anything else to say. If my Italian was so incomprehensible, how was Aunt Giulia able to understand me? She started talking again, and I listened to her. Aunt Felicetta had a kind of sour expression on her face. In fact, the corner of her mouth turned down in a very familiar way.

Oh my God. Connie.

The understanding of DNA was not yet a part of our collective knowledge, but at that moment the mysteries of genetics were laid bare before me. Had I been a scientist, I would have been fascinated. As someone who simply wanted to get away from home, however, I was somewhere between apprehensive and downright horrified! I realized before too many days had passed that I had learned a language and traveled 6,000 miles just to be dominated by two women again: one who doted on me, and one who tormented me.

I made lots of friends quickly and spent as much time as I could going out with them, visiting people and places and giving Aunt Felicetta little opportunity to nag. Everyone knew the two sisters who lived in the center of town, and people were quite frank about Felicetta's disagreeable personality. As much as everyone liked Giulia, most conceded that they didn't really care for Felicetta. Aunt Guilia told me privately that Felicetta took her personality from their mother. I had always heard from Grandma that the reason Great-Grandpa didn't return to his wife was that she was "crabby". It was only now that I realized that she was Connie's namesake—Grandpa had named Connie for his mother, Concetta. Connie always hated her name, I knew, and had gone by "Connie" since childhood.

I also learned that no one was above DNA. Several old women in the village called me *Pietro recarnate* ("Pietro reincarnated"), and *Pietro resuscitato* ("Pietro revived"). Apparently I looked just like Grandpa's father, whose picture I had never seen. When I asked Aunt Giulia about it, she produced a photograph, and sure enough it looked like me. Small wonder she smothered me with affection. I was not only a surrogate for seeing her brother again, but also her father, whom she last saw when he was a young man and she was around eight years old.

Giulia had never married.   She was around seventy. Felicetta, four years older, was widowed. The two had run a little one-room general store in the front of the house, which they apparently opened now only by appointment. I saw no new stock being delivered, so I assumed they were just slowly selling off old inventory when they could.

A couple bickering sisters four years apart in age, and a run-down store. What else was new?

Collelongo itself was a captivating place. High up in the mountains about seventy miles from Rome, it was a small village of some 250 people.   There were only three telephones in the town.   One was in the mayor's office/ police station; another was in the telegraph office. The third was in a bar.

Everyone cooked and heated with wood stoves, so the town smelled as though it had been freshly grilled. It was a pleasant enough fragrance. To this day, when I smell wood smoke I still think of Italy.

Collelongo had stone and stucco buildings and elaborate brick work in the piazzas, as one would expect in Italy. For a poor country place, they didn't skimp on masonry. Small wonder Great-Grandpa was a stonemason. I once expressed my awe to my cousin Marco that Aunt Giulia and Aunt Felicetta's house had all marble floors. He sniffed, pointed toward the north, and said, "The *whole mountain* is marble." Meaning, of course, that value was rooted in scarcity, and marble was not scarce here. I thought of the old story about the man in the desert exchanging a bag of diamonds for a drink of water.

Living in a country place for the first time in my life took some getting used to. Like the Old-McDonald-had-a-farm stereotype, a rooster would wake me up every morning— earlier than I wanted—and it was charming for the first few days. Then it was a real pain. If I had been on a real farm I might have accepted it, but the damn bird would position itself under my window in the alley just off the main street of the town. I went out on the balcony and looked down at him. "Hey, Signor Gallo!" I shouted. "Shut the hell up!" I knew it wouldn't do any good but it felt better that I said it.

It was a couple weeks after I had arrived that I got to see for the first time the true ancestral home. Giulia and Felicetta now lived in the house where Felicetta and her husband had lived before he died. The place where they grew up was a five-minute walk away. They rented most of the building and that gave them some kind of income.

It was a three-story masonry building that contained several apartments. My great-grandfather had built it himself. Aunt Giulia took me into the place where he had lived. There was no electricity. This was an o-o-old place. We walked around with candles in the middle of the day. Empty houses are a little spooky. Empty houses of European design are more unsettling to an American, I think, because they are so foreign. But an empty Italian house of the late 19th Century is seriously creepy—especially with the ghosts of that cantankerous DNA oozing out of the cracked plaster walls! *If it was nighttime and I was here alone, some female ghost would start arguing with me*, I thought.

But providing a contrast to all the antiquities was my coterie of young friends. I had one male friend, Gino; but I had a surplus of pretty girls who escorted me most places. The group was distilled into four regulars: Ascenza, Tonina, Tecla, and Antonina. One of my favorite movies in the '60s was *Our Man Flint*, about an improbable super secret agent with four girlfriends. I was in my glory, parading around with four girls who were crazy about me. I was getting back that feeling of being master of my fate.

Taking more than my share of the female populace naturally caused some resentment among the local chaps. One night, I was in a bar with Gino and a couple guys were clearly hostile toward me. One kept asking me why I wasn't in the army. I explained that my lottery number was too high to be called—at that time, we were issued random numbers in the U.S. and only numbers one through fifty were being called for the draft. He either didn't get it, or didn't accept it. I didn't realize at that time that military service was mandatory in Italy. All males my age served two years. But that wasn't really the issue.

Sure enough, the two were waiting when I left. They confronted me there in the narrow alleyway, and I prepared for trouble. With five years of karate training behind me at that time, it was natural to just drop my weight down and assume a fighting stance—accompanied by a hair-raising yell. The two bolted like deer. One screamed "Karateeeeee!" as he ran. Thanks to my being from somewhere else—and what might be called "advance publicity" on the part of Our Man Flint, James Bond, and other movie characters who hacked their way though mobs of attackers with their hands and feet—I was saved the need of actually using my punches and kicks. After that, the men in the small town left me alone. Alone with my four girlfriends.

They weren't girlfriends in the sense of lovers, really; Tonina was said to have a boyfriend, but I never saw him. She would join us most of the time. There was a fifth girl named Maria Chiara, a hanger-on who did in fact have a boyfriend and was never physically affectionate with me but nonetheless wanted to spend some time around The American.

We went on day trips around the province on weekends, and took walks in the evenings in the little town, talking and laughing and exchanging knowledge about our respective countries. I would hold hands with two of them in shifts, switching to the other two on the way back. I noticed Antonina's hand alone would be sweaty. Then I wondered if it was mine that was sweating. But it didn't matter. It only happened with her.

She looked at me differently. There were lots of shy glances and when we faced each other, there was a soulful look that made it clear that something very different was going on with her. I advanced to the arm-around-the-shoulder posture when walking with her. There was no sign of jealousy on the part of the other three. *Try that in America*, I thought to myself.

Antonina's goodnight kiss was also different from the others'. I found myself really starting to fall in love with her. But back home I had a girlfriend, one I had been pretty serious about. What was I doing?

Hmmm. Back home. As good a time as I was having, I felt a nagging pull back home. It was a vague sense of disquiet, like remembering homework you haven't done, on a Sunday night. I suddenly had more of a desire to get my life going than I ever experienced at college. And yet, what was it that I wanted? It certainly wasn't a bunch of boring classes and an eventual career I didn't ask for.

I announced my intent to leave (*after* making my arrangements—I learned the order in which to do things with my family back home) and my aunts were crestfallen. Antonina was disconsolate and I was secretly happy that she cared that much, but yet confused about what I wanted. When we said our goodbyes, she squeezed my hand tightly and I didn't think she would let go.

But I had a mission of some kind; undefined, even fuzzy, but most definitely felt. That need to return was nagging. It was like graduating school and being anxious to join the work force—except that I hadn't graduated, and had only the vaguest ideas about what I wanted to do for a career. Still, I felt that the experience in "the old country" had been an education of some sort, and I had certainly graduated if I felt like I had.

On the morning I was to leave, I spotted "Signor Gallo" the rooster out in the alley, pecking on some odds and ends between the bricks. I walked over, briskly, and got surprisingly close before he started waddling away. He was too late. I booted him in the tail feathers and he left the earth for a brief time. It was very satisfying.

Much more could be written about my Italian chapter but its main value in this narrative, as well as in my life, is its relationship to my life in America. As an influence, as an aspect of my heritage, and as an event that touched not only my life but my grandfather's as well.

I pondered all this on the long trip back. More so than on the voyage over, I now had a strong sense of being emissary for the Negri family that settled in the New World. I was also returning to my home as a world-traveled and cultured man (I believed! Ha!). Our Man Flint, indeed.

Arriving in New York, I had a layover before catching the next plane for home. I stopped at a pay phone and looked at the directory.   It was huge!   The disparity between Morgantown's phone book and Manhattan's drove home the size of the place. I thumbed through the listings and found my father's name. I took a deep breath, put a dime in the slot, and called him.

I was ready to hang up the phone out of sheer nervousness when a voice said, "Hello?" It was a voice I remembered. A baritone of medium timbre, resonant, that somehow did not conjure visions of uneasy dinners, toy planes that didn't fly, or anything uncomfortable at all. If anything, it brought back dim memories of infanthood, when everything was new and positive; not the man who was the opposite of the family I knew. In a few short minutes, I had accepted unconsciously that this voice belonged to someone I wanted to know, now.

I gave him my flight information and he said he would try to get there to see me off. JFK Airport was the largest place I had ever seen at that time. It was immense. Once I hung up the phone and looked around, I wondered how in the world two people were going to find each other in this huge arena with hundreds of people jostling each other and no view of the street doors.

Time passed and it was nearing time for me to board my flight. Still too inexperienced to feel any sense of panic, I stayed at the spot I had told him, and presently, a rain coated figure elbowed his way through impatient travelers who were moving *en masse* in the opposite direction. Even at such a distance, of both space and years, I recognized my father. He looked about, with a harried look on his face. I waved.

And then there he was before me. *Yes*, I thought, *I remember this man.* I recognized the eyes, and that little freckle on the tip of his nose. I remembered more things than I could have seen in the small, fuzzy, black-and-white images of the TV at home. I didn't even realize he was talking while I was filing back though my memories of childhood. I told him of my travels, and it was he who initiated my rush to the boarding gate. A nerve-wracking taxi ride for him to the airport and what must have been a minute-and-a-half reunion dampened the awkwardness for both of us. We embraced and I promised to keep in touch. His eyes were laughing as I turned and waved again before heading through the doorway, urged on by the stewardess. Dad. *My Dad.*

The flight was short. Another plane—small, a commuter—deposited me right back where I started. I didn't feel prepared to be back now. Mom picked me up at the airport and friction started almost immediately.

18

I told everyone about my adventures in Italy, conveyed messages from my aunts to my grandfather, and waited a week for my film to be developed. Finally, the awaited glimpses of the Old World were shared by everyone in the family, and Grandpa was happy to see them. There was one picture of his sisters looking kind of mournful and I explained to him that I took it before leaving for the airport. He asked me a surprising and insightful question: "Did you feel like you were going home or leaving it?" I really didn't know. I certainly felt both; what proportions, though, I couldn't tell.

He and I talked more often then about family history. I learned that the given name of the first male alternated with the generations. Grandpa's name was Bartolo. His father's was Pietro. Pietro's father's name was Bartolomeo, and his father in turn was named Pietro.

But Grandpa had two daughters and the tradition ended. "I wanted you to be named Pietro," he said, "but...*ehhh!*" It was a non-word, an expression of mild disgust that I recognized.

I told him I finally saw a picture of Great-grandpa. He said, "My father had a real nice moustache." I had been wearing one myself for two years, never thinking about any familial significance, of course, since I had been inspired to grow it by seeing how cool Robert Redford looked with one in "Butch Cassidy and the Sundance Kid". Now I knew why Grandpa was the only one in the house who hadn't given me a hard time about growing it.

I noticed over the next few days that he seemed to have shaved poorly. He often went a few days without shaving at that point, but this was different. Then the hair began to show more prominently on his upper lip. *By golly*, I thought, *he's growing a moustache*. He didn't say anything to me about it, but I knew from our conversation, and the way he described his father's *real nice moustache*, what was up. I overheard Mom one evening in the living room telling him to shave more carefully. I didn't hear him give any response. When she came into the kitchen I said, chuckling, "He's growing a moustache."

"He is *not!*" she said, not in a disbelieving sense but in an authoritative one. He *will* not. The next day, he was clean-shaven. I felt bad.

One day soon after, we were alone in the house and he was sitting in the living room when I came in. He gestured toward the television. "Turn that thing off, will you?" he asked. I had had some run-in with Connie earlier and mentioned that, and he became pensive. I changed the subject and started talking about something else, but he began a narrative as though he hadn't heard what I said.

"When Eleanor was a baby," he said, "there were some people come over." He never referred to her as "Mom", or "your mother" to me—a curious thing. "Eleanor was just born, and Connie was four."

He was looking across the room as if reliving the event. "We put the baby in a bassinette in another room, to sleep. Everybody was sitting around talking, and in a little bit I went in to check on the baby. Connie was bending over the baby. She had her hands around the baby's throat. She was jealous of the baby, you see."

Holy cats! A homicidal four year-old?

He turned toward me. "She was choking the baby. I slapped her across the face like this"—and here he made a crying face to imitate the jealous sister that was both humorous and pathetic at the same time. "All the attention was going to the new baby, you see." He looked back at the distant wall.

The story didn't surprise me, given my long history of conflict with Connie, but it helped me understand things a little better. I realized for the first time that who we are and what we are could be established very, very early. And for some people, that essence would never change. Maybe for most people.

Grandpa soon had another bad episode with his health that necessitated his going to the hospital. When Mom told me the ambulance was coming, I thought back to his last hospitalization, which had not been long before.

It had been an ominous scene when he called all of us into his hospital room and gave what amounted to his end-of-life speech. It was fresh in my memory. "I've lived a good life," he said, "and I have the sweetest family a man could have." Grandma sat there with a peculiar look on her face; a smile that wasn't a smile. Connie was crying, periodically blurting out, "Daddy, don't!" I was clueless. I had never experienced the death of anyone close to me, and had no real understanding of Grandpa's medical condition. No one discussed it with me, except to say that "fluid was building up in his body." That certainly didn't tell me anything that I could process. I remember looking down at him in his bed and not knowing what to think at all.

Yet, he returned to us after a week or so and the crisis was over and almost forgotten (at least by me). He had been back in his chair in the living room and telling me about his father's moustache and all manner of interesting family stuff, and now the threat of losing him was real again? I felt a little panic setting in as the two burly men went up to his bedroom, put him in a kitchen chair, and carried him down the stairs—vertically—to the front door.

But my panic was dispelled quickly. Whereas the previous trip to the hospital had had a grim atmosphere, Grandpa made light of it this time. "Oh, I'm going for a ride?" he joked with the ambulance drivers as they hoisted him in the chair. He seemed unfazed. As he passed by me, he said, "I'll be back in a coupla days."

I had it on authority that he would be back. I didn't worry.

The next morning, I was washing my face when I heard the phone ring. Connie was upstairs and answered it. A minute later, she yanked open the door to my basement room. "The hospital just phoned," she called out in a shaky voice. "They say Grandpa's worse."

I was standing near the phone in my room when it rang again. I answered. It was Mom. She started talking when I heard the click of the upstairs extension. Connie got on the phone and told Mom the same thing she had just told me. "Connie," she replied, "Daddy died."

Connie began bawling loudly and Mom continued to talk to me, calmly. She was going to the store to tell Grandma. I was to go to the hospital and wait for them. I hung up the phone and bent over to put my shoes on and felt like the room was spinning. I ran out the door with my shoes still untied, ran down the block to the hospital and found a nurse who was expecting me. She showed me to his room.

He was not breathing when I went into the room, but then why would I expect him to be? *Come on, come on, say it. "Cristofero, d'joo eat?"* He didn't say anything. He lay there with his hands folded over his midriff, as they are all supposed to look. Some nurse had probably placed them that way when she detected no heartbeat. He was still wearing his long underwear that he had been wearing in his bedroom. I spoke to him, bending over closely. I thought his eyes opened for a brief second and closed again. *Come on, please say it.* I collapsed with grief onto his chest, crying and holding onto him. I remember how hollow his body sounded when I fell on it. As if there was nothing inside anymore, not even any organs; just air. That's when I really knew.

I can draw from all my knowledge of anatomy and physiology now, years later, and I can tell you about the last little bit of air retained by the lungs in the midst of that vacuum, and the stasis of blood in the connective tissue, and the last neurological impulses that can do things like run the automatic functions long after no one's home. But I didn't need any education to know from that sound that no one was home anymore.

I was devastated. And more than a little disoriented. But I was there. No one else was there. The nurses outside let me have my private time, then offered me tranquilizers as I waited for my mother to arrive. I didn't take them. Connie had arrived, and sat crying on a chair in the hall. The nurses walked briskly past with their squeaky shoes on the tile floor. The bench I sat on squeaked also, as I leaned forward and looked at the floor. Connie cried harder and louder and it echoed down the hall. A patient came out of his room in a bathrobe to look and I recognized him as the man who owned the gas station where Mom took her car. It was the only time I ever saw him not smiling.

I thought about that old baritone horn, how I'd planned to clean it up and surprise Grandpa with it. It was like waiting until the last minute to choose my major. Always too late. Always too late.

It was the worst thing that had ever happened to me.

Two days later, I was at the funeral home awaiting the end of visitation before going to the cemetery for the interment. I was holding up pretty well. Grandma was holding up well. Mom was her ever-efficient and controlled self. Connie was dramatic, of course. Everyone was pretty much the way they always were. Then in walked Tony Colasante, the old Italian man—older than Grandpa—who had been around forever and for whom I had called countless taxis. I never saw such profound grief on a human face, before or since. I distracted myself talking to Gianghetto, who had come in from Ohio to be one of the pallbearers. I couldn't look at Tony.

Once more, the command came from Grandma: "Call Tony a cab." I called him a cab from a phone in the hall. I didn't feel so good now. I went out on the diminutive porch of the funeral home, and was followed by Tony in a minute. He looked at me, the same expression on his face, and said, "I'm awful-a sorry."

The old man and I stood there, waiting for the taxi, and just cried. We cried *torrents*. The cab finally came and I helped him in. I watched it drive away and thought, *This is the worst stinking day of my life.*

19

With Grandpa gone, there was no longer any unifying force within the Negri household. He was the most important thing any of us had in common. I didn't realize it at the time, but it became pretty evident that something essential was missing because from that time on, we were a bunch of individual souls clashing under a common roof.

Having disappointed my mother with my aborted journalism college experience, she was completely unsympathetic with the prospective careers I preferred. There was no indulging my wanting to learn other things. I wasn't an active student, therefore I should get a job. I was being a bum. So I ran through a number of short-term jobs that ranged from embarrassing to downright awful. I was a door-to-door salesman. I worked in fast food restaurants. I weighed trucks and bagged sand at an asphalt plant. I stocked shelves in a market (at least I knew how to do that). I even dug graves. That one didn't last too long.

But two things, two life-changing things, happened. Finally a legal adult, I got a sympathetic lawyer and petitioned the court to change my name. Mom was furious, but she was furious about nearly everything I did at that time. It didn't matter to me. I was once again master of my fate. I changed my middle name to Pietro and my last name to Negri. *Hey Grandpa, the tradition continues!*

I realized some time later that Mom's opposition to my name change must have been at least partly based on the fact that, with us having different last names (she had kept my father's), it made it appear as though I had been an illegitimate child. I hadn't considered that my having her maiden name might have been embarrassing for her, but she didn't communicate her reasoning to me. Sitting down and rationally explaining one's thinking was definitely *not* a Negri family tradition. If she had explained it in those terms, I might have had second thoughts, but anger was all I received. It seemed that they thought anger was the only way to be heard in that house. I was sick of the yelling and anxious to get out and have my own life. And I figured they were still making plenty of people named Lamb on my father's side. Without me, the Negri family line would end.

The second life-changing thing that happened is that I developed a couple health problems that opened up a new world for me. With a chronically stiff neck and a strange condition that was slowly robbing me of my vision—two problems I thought unrelated—I called upon Doctor Miller of the City Market. He was retired but still saw patients in a small office in his home. The man I had watched drink his after-work bottle of beer for years was now my doctor.

Explaining the concepts of Osteopathy to me as he restored the range of motion in my neck, it became more obvious to me that these concepts were true, for my vision was clearing as well. It was a school of medicine that emphasized the unity of the body, and recognized the musculoskeletal system as being involved with organic functioning. He explained that the nerve impingement and restricted blood flow caused by the mechanical misalignment in my spine had caused the problem with my eyes. I had the proof of the pudding. I could see better than I had in a year. The medical doctors I had seen didn't do anything for me.

Manipulation of the spine and muscles can do this? It was nothing short of amazing. When I read that the traditional osteopath had a mostly drugless practice, I thought about the line of pill bottles on the kitchen counter that Grandpa had taken every day. What if those pills had hastened, rather than postponed, his death? There was something very appealing about the idea of healing without drugs, and I began studying up on natural medicine. It was amusing, and yet not surprising, that my ultimate choice of career was spurred by a City Market regular.

Doctor Miller tried to persuade me to go to osteopathic medical school. A chiropractor I had met at the time begged me to go to chiropractic school. "Osteopaths don't learn all that anymore," he told me, "they use synthetic drugs just like MDs." Well, that was disheartening. Doctor Miller was one of the last of a breed, which was obvious even to me. Was there much of a difference in the ways osteopaths and chiropractors used their hands? So many questions to be answered. I was intensely interested.

Naturopathic medicine was of great interest to me but the profession had declined to the point that there was only one school left that I could find, and it was just an impossible proposition. "Naturopaths are a dying breed," said Doctor Miller.

Then I learned that the various manual methods that we associated with these schools in the West were present in the medical methods of the Far East. Soft tissue and joint manipulation had been employed in traditional "Oriental medicine" for centuries. It was at this point in time that the American public had its first look at the most dramatic tool in Asian medicine—acupuncture. It looked as though this was an up-and-coming field, and it meshed perfectly with my philosophy. I made my choice. I would study Oriental medicine.

At that point in time, though, there were far fewer schools of Oriental medicine than Chiropractic or Osteopathy. But I was able to etch out a workable plan that allowed me to do training one trimester at a time with a school in Florida. They had a modular format, so that you could complete the training at any pace. I could sit out a trimester, make some more money, and resume my training. I would not have that luxury with any other school. And it was necessary, because in those days there were no educational loans for such training.

A course that would apply to my studies was available in New York City. I was anxious to take it, but it probably would not have been possible if my father had not offered to let me stay with him. Once again I was getting off a plane in New York, and began getting to know my father at once.

His little apartment on East 57th Street looked just as I had imagined a New York apartment. A tiny kitchen, made all the more tiny by the presence of a butcher block that doubled as a countertop; a dining area in the living room composed of a small round table and two canvas director's chairs; a hide-a-bed couch. Dad's easel with a half-finished painting on it, leaning against a wall. A wooden drawing mannequin stood on a windowsill, seeming to look at the painting. Two windows looked out on a courtyard with some greenery. Nice.

It smelled of tobacco smoke and hair oil and a man. I was in a different world.

Dad fixed dinner, served it, poured wine. We talked for hours. My butt got numb. The good thing about the canvas chair was that you could reach underneath and scratch when you wanted to, without having to stand up.

I told him about all the events of recent months. He was sentimental about Grandpa. "Poor old guy," he said, "I always liked him. He just wanted to be in his little store away from a house of screaming women." After an absence of twenty years, Dad still had an accurate picture.

I thought about the irony of changing my name to Negri, then seeking a relationship with my father. The irony of that was not lost on Dad, who cocked his head back, raised an eyebrow, made a *faux*-imperious look, and said, "You *might* have kept my name."

"Don't worry about that. I love you, Dad."

"I love you too, son."

I would have a father again, for the next twenty years.

Afterword

It would take me six years to complete my schooling in my piecemeal fashion. The City Market, run for a time by Grandma and Connie, closed. I began my career in natural medicine and my world shifted away from the beery universe of oddball characters, low-rent locales, and colorful vernacular.

Over the years, I have achieved a second doctorate degree, had eight medical books published, and have recently semi-retired after 46 years in practice. I have moved back to downtown Morgantown (having closed an office in Pittsburgh), and the old familiar sights cause me to look around for City Market customers when I travel the sidewalks. But there are none of the old characters that I remember left to walk the streets.

In the pre-modern era, a market was a hub of society; it not only provided sustenance but also the town gossip, social interaction, and a (respectable) place to go. The concept of "market" is still so essential that we refer to commerce and the economy as the "marketplace"—it implies knowledge of what people are concerned with and doing. The City Market lived up to its name, after all. It was not just a place to buy groceries. It was a gathering place; it was a microcosm of society. The people who came to the City Market had the same varied dreams—sometimes accomplished, often not—as the rest of the populace. They brought with them the same anger, the same hilarity, the same bemused philosophical fatalism, even the same horrors. Businessman, cleaning woman, laborer, unemployed drunk —they were no different. They each had something interesting to impart and never, even at their very worst, was completely devoid of dignity. What they *might have been* is irrelevant. What they ended up being, and what they meant to me, is the story of the City Market.

What Yours Truly might have been is now irrelevant as well. I am struck by the fact that I have written technical books, and now a biographical book (and in fact a large body of essays and creative writing), *after dismissing a degree in journalism* all those years ago. Mom may have had foresight. It is also strange to realize that I am now the retirement-aged Doctor Miller of my generation, stopping on my way home for a glass of beer, at someone else's bar.

No one in the bar is ever very interesting. I've been spoiled, you see.

The beer tap in the foreground, finally dry, looks on as sundry items are cleared off the back bar. In the mirror, Mom talks to Nick the Greek Man, in a surreal shot as the City Market is dismantled.

A last look at the City Market.

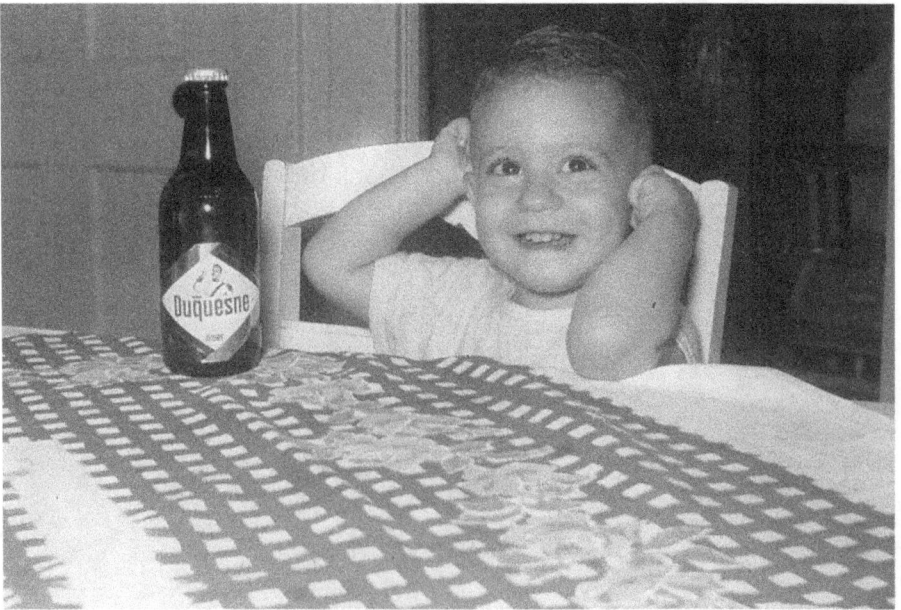

The author, "at his peak". He still drinks
Duquesne, when he can get it.